Shortlisted for ...
Shortlisted for the E...
The Times Nat... ... 2019

'Brilliant memoir about nature, landscape, food and the disconnect between town and country.'

India Knight, *The Sunday Times*

'Even when it has all been swallowed by the sea, the art [the Suffolk landscape] has helped create will survive - and Blaxland's book deserves a distinguished place in that company.'

The Telegraph

'I feel like a stalker, but reading Juliet Blaxland's *The Easternmost House*, I got straight into my car and drove over to stare at her home. Her wonderful book describes living on the most extreme outpost of Suffolk's coast of erosion.'

Janice Turner, *The Times*

'The author writes beautifully about her life in this small extremity ... a hymn to a simpler life, one lived more in tune with the rhythms of the natural world, with its wonders and its perils.'

Country Life

'A marvellous evocation of the Suffolk coast. It made me want to jump on the next train out of London.'

Andrew Gimson, author of *Gimson's Kings & Queens*

Juliet Blaxland is an architect, author, cartoonist and illustrator. She is the author and illustrator of twelve children's books, and a prize-winning photographer. She grew up in a remote part of Suffolk and now lives on a crumbling cliff at the easternmost edge of England.

THE
EASTERNMOST
HOUSE

A Year of Life on the Edge of England

JULIET BLAXLAND

SANDSTONE PRESS

First published in Great Britain by
Sandstone Press Ltd
Dochcarty Road
Dingwall
Ross-shire
IV15 9UG
Scotland

www.sandstonepress.com

The publisher acknowledges subsidy from Creative Scotland
towards publication of this volume.

ISBN: 978-1-912240-54-8
ISBNe: 978-1-912240-55-5

Cover design by David Eldridge
Typeset by Iolaire Typography Ltd, Newtonmore
Printed and bound by CPI Group (UK) Ltd, Croydon, CR0 4YY

The Easternmost House is dedicated to all the people who have been physically involved in the making of the British landscape in the past, and to those who still live and work in the countryside or on the land today: farmers, fishermen, shepherds, hedge layers, thatchers, stone wallers, flint knappers, barn builders, farriers, racehorse trainers, grooms, vets, pub landlords, village shopkeepers, butchers, tractor drivers, 'fellows who cut the hay', fruit pickers, gardeners, tree planters, landowners, river keepers, ghillies and everyone else not yet mentioned . . .

I am also very grateful to Jane Graham-Maw of Graham-Maw Christie, literary agent, Moira Forsyth of Sandstone Press, publisher, John Lewis-Stempel, author and *Country Life* columnist, and Giles Stibbe, husband, for their belief in this book before it really existed.

Twitter @JulietBlaxland
#TheEasternmostHouse

'The great thing about Suffolk is that once you arrive here, you are in a kind of simple environment, a comfortable, gorgeous place, where the people will be delightful and friendly. They don't go off to wild lives or other distractions with noise and traffic. There is also the way it looks. It's such a beautiful county. If you live here, you get really used to the unbelievable beaches, the curve of the land, the beauty of the villages.

If you are making a film about England, you can find everything you want, and more, here.'

Richard Curtis, on filming in Suffolk
June 2018

CONTENTS

The world today is sick to its thin blood for lack of elemental things, for fire before the hands, for water welling up from the earth, for air, for the dear earth itself underfoot.

Henry Beston
The Outermost House, 1928

INFLUENCES

I live in a house on a windblown clifftop at the easternmost edge of what used to be the easternmost parish of England. The church fell into the sea in 1666, and this house – itself called the Easternmost House – has possibly only three summers left before it too is lost to coastal erosion. I wanted to describe a year of life on this crumbling cliff at the easternmost edge of England, in all seasons and in all weathers. This 'year of life' is in fact the distillation of several years of life. There are stories, and beginnings, middles and ends, but not necessarily in that order.

We live here all year round, and have done so for several years, but I cannot say how many, for fear that to do so might itself tempt fate to render our life here episodic or experimental, and to end it with the destruction of the cliff and our house in a sudden storm.

Two nature-writing classics in particular are the ancestors of this book. The first is *The Outermost*

House, by Henry Beston, first published in 1928, which takes as its subject a year of life on the great beach at Cape Cod. The second is *Ring of Bright Water*, by Gavin Maxwell, first published in 1959, which is about much more than the otters for which it will always be remembered. In each of these two books, the actual lives lived were the main adventure, and the writing was the offspring of the life. In each, there is also a deliberate attempt to live away from the mass of humanity, and to relate more closely to the natural world. Both also share an unspoken renunciation of the values of an urbanised society, and of materialism for its own sake. I suspect that Henry Beston's lament that the world is 'sick for lack of elemental things' must be even truer today than it was in 1928. Gavin Maxwell's assertion that places such as Camusfearna in Scotland are symbols of freedom from the 'prison of over-dense communities' and the 'incarceration of office walls and hours' echoes Beston's discomfort, but thirty years later. To their perceived horrors of the modern world as it was then, we can add a panoply of new ones: overpopulation, social media, plastic, pylons, sprawl.

Xanadu, Shangri-La, Tir na n'Og, Avalon, Camusfearna, Arcadia. These names are all evocations of an archetype of an idyll, an earthly paradise set in a landscape of natural beauty, sometimes a place of myth or mystery. A suitable dwelling for such a scene might be a temple folly set in acres of rolling parkland, a timber cabin in a forest, a whitewashed cottage in a rugged landscape of rock and sea. But these places exist primarily in the imagination, so they can be changed, adjusted and revisited at will.

The Easternmost House is our real-life version, and throughout this book I will try to make this place as real to you as it is to us, and to convey some of the natural wonders surrounding us in this magical landscape of light and sky and water.

Look to this day!
For it is life, the very life of life.
Look well, therefore, to this day!
Such is the salutation of the dawn.

Ancient Sanskrit Poem

INTRODUCTION

I had a rural 1970s childhood. Much of it was spent in what would now be seen as significant physical danger, often in literal and social isolation, sometimes with only animals for company, but all of which was normal for the time and place. My sister was older, earnest and bookish, and the noisier tribe of cousins and friends lived several miles or counties away, so I invented some imaginary brothers for everyday company, and to liven things up. I was also a tomboy, and for a time I privately self-identified as a dun pony.

It was a world in which death and disaster were ever-present. Drownings, broken bones, chainsaw incidents, fires, injuries by farm machinery and rogue elements of buildings, tramplings by beware-of-the-bulls and/or motherly cows protecting calves, were regular, if not quite commonplace.

There were also countless separate dramas involving ponies, including one in which I was caught in a thunderstorm in a wide-open landscape, and had to decide how not to be struck by lightning. With hindsight, I should have led the pony into an isolated church on our route, which would have had a lightning conductor on its tower and offered a little flint fortress of physical protection. But as I was only eleven and operating in a slightly more God-fearing era than now, the leading-the-pony-into-the-church option passed me by. In the event, I took a direct line across the country in the manner of a nineteenth-century hunting print, and just galloped home.

I invented methods for combatting my everyday dangers and demons. The dangers were self-evident, and my demons were the more emotional, invisible side of things, such as having to go reluctantly back to boarding school seven counties away, from the age of ten, or not crying when guinea pigs and dogs and ponies, and eventually people, died of old age.

Having settled into an inescapably odd boarding-school routine of Latin tests and fencing practice during term time (as in sword-fighting, not creosote), punctuated by the rural rhythms of being barked at by tweedy retired colonels in various horse-related contexts in the holidays, by the time I reached my eleventh birthday I would have been perfectly equipped for a life in the Household Cavalry.

I know in reality that for much of the time as a child I was either cold, wet, frightened or mildly unhappy, yet the distilled memory is of one perpetual summer holiday, magically set in the long, hot summer of 1976. This trick of human memory is one of nature's small miracles, a talismanic nugget to hold on to for life.

I got away quite lightly, in terms of horse-related-injury, but in one teenage incident I suffered a head injury which I believe may have changed my brain and the way I think. I became more extreme and lateral-thinking and drawn to a new world, of Rothko and Miro and Brutalism and Deconstructivism, and curious about anything else that seemed unfamiliar, edgy, incomprehensible or just interesting. Perhaps this set me on a path to the architect and architectural cartoonist that I eventually became. These small but potentially life-changing dramas were considered completely unremarkable in the rural context of that time.

Later, when I lived in London, I realised that my habitual and evidently necessary rural alertness had translated itself to coping with the hazards of city life. Instead of looking out for falling branches, I would cross the road to avoid scaffolding in a high wind. Instead of being wary of being kicked by a horse by assessing its body language, I would scan the mean streets of London for potential murderers and muggers by reading the same uneasy signs. I never did acclimatise to traffic, which appears to me as a river full of crocodiles would to a zebra foal. One day, the scaffolding near our office actually did fall down.

So when I eventually returned to my rural roots and the familiar Suffolk landscape as an adult, living and working – as many country people do – often outside, often alone, often up a ladder, chopping wood with an axe, climbing around an old building, dealing with large and excitable animals, planting trees, tending bonfires, or otherwise being in some degree of danger which rarely arises in an office, I found that what I had always thought of as my tomboy habits actually turned out to be useful training for our life on the cliff.

The *haar* is an eerie sea-fog which cloaks our cliff and renders the edge invisible. On one such foggy day, when my soldier husband Giles was in a war zone in Afghanistan, I turned for home down our track and saw at the end, near the edge, the ghostly figures of two men. Instantly I assumed they must be army Welfare Officers. As I passed the farm buildings, I had already imagined that Giles had 'life-changing injuries'. By the time I reached the opening in the hedge by the metal gate, I had the idea that he had 'not survived his injuries'. As I reached the end of the track and the cliff-edge, so that the men became bigger and nearer, I could see that they both held clipboards.

We had been briefed about the protocol of such things in a little book, including what happens when something happens to 'your soldier'. IED. Improvised Explosive Device. Invisible. Lethal. Life-changing. Fatal. So sorry. Not survived. In that short distance these phrases became seared onto my brain as blackly as if they had been burnt on with a branding iron. Now these two harmless grey figures had come to tell me I would now be alone, properly alone, forever.

I had heard from somewhere that people who are on the receiving end of sudden bad news, of a death in a car crash, of a suicide, or of instant widowhood at the hands of an IED, often make it even more difficult for the bearers of the bad news, by not taking in the message. People are in denial. They do not fully comprehend that what has happened, has happened. So, as I trundled up the track towards these misty grim reapers, I rehearsed how I would sit them down and offer them a cup of coffee. I would tell them that I had heard about this bad-news-denial syndrome. I would reassure them that I understood, that death was to be half-expected when you are in the army. That modern soldiers of all ranks have chosen their job, or at least their vocation. That the stiff upper lip has served us well and thank you, yes, I will be fine absolutely. But even these carefully-marshalled thoughts were already beginning to become muddled.

The grey men were by now very close, so I stiffened the sinews and summoned up the blood to speak to them. Or at least try to listen to them. They mumbled a reply, the fragmented gist of which included a grey fog of dull corporate words: 'Council . . . engagement . . . team . . . assessing . . . the progress . . . of coastal erosion . . .'

Assessing the progress of coastal erosion . . . I could have pushed them off the cliff.

I could have explained about the IED and the emotional *haar* that had just engulfed me. But distant echoes of wartime grandparents, Nimrod at the Cenotaph, tweedy colonels and all our unfashionable old-school training somehow conspire to suppress any outward show of emotion at times of crisis, so I just smiled sweetly and offered them a cup of coffee as planned. The council engagement team looked mildly surprised at this unexpectedly random hospitality, but chattily enjoyed two mugs of instant coffee each, looking out to sea, and then shuffled off into their logo-ed van with a few cheerfully engaging small-talk remarks about what an odd place to live, etcetera. And what odd people, no doubt, not far away in their thoughts.

Giles was, for the moment, safe. But this house was very much not.

People have often asked what it is like to be an army wife alone on a cliff with a husband away in a war zone and how you avoid being overwhelmed with loneliness and anxiety. I have never been lonely when alone. What makes me lonely is people asking if I am lonely and what makes me anxious is people asking if I am anxious. My antidote to loneliness and anxiety is to have physically and/or mentally engaging projects. In my London days, I used to engage in guerilla gardening and gritty urban photography tours on my bike and spent long afternoons helping with a group of volunteers taking disabled people for rides on very quiet horses and ponies of appropriate size and sweetness. Now, I might build a chicken run, plant a kitchen garden, clip a hedge or rescue a greyhound. Anyone who lives in the country knows that there is also a constant need to engage in what might be called 'unprofessional mass catering', for causes or committees, guests or glut-processing reasons.

Reading about the source of the anxiety helps, in this case Afghanistan. The thing about war zones is you never know when they are safe. Soldiers in any war are sometimes safe. They know when they are safe, but we at home do not. Constant anxiety, both here and there, becomes normal and familiar for the whole six months, until the plane lands. The other thing about war zones is that everyone else is going about their civilian daily business *not* thinking about war zones, so you keep your war-zone thoughts in a separate bubble, much as I imagine you might keep your deeply-religious thoughts or your bank-robbing thoughts in a separate bubble, at least when in the company of people who might not share or understand them.

Conversely, *we* are sometimes in danger, while those in the war zone think of home as perpetually cosy and safe. I know that when I walk alone on our beach, if something happened to me, I would probably not be rescued, at least not in time. Therefore, thinking back to that list of rural disasters, I deliberately remind myself that it is up to me, and me alone, to be watchful and have imagination about what sort of 'something' might happen, and where I place myself, and whether this is a safe place to put my feet, and whether this wet sinking sand is going to swallow me up, and so on. It becomes second nature.

Once, a large branch of a tree narrowly missed crashing down on a person as she rode her bicycle up the drive when I was a child. More recently, a visitor was killed, buried by a cliff fall a few miles to the south of us. When a report appeared in the paper, of people desperately trying to rescue this person and a dog with their bare hands, a detail that was not mentioned but which was visible in the picture, was that the tide was high so the beach was narrow. Now, when I walk on the beach alone,

I do a rough mental calculation that there is enough beach to equal the height of the cliff, and I walk beyond the imagined height-line on the beach. If the tide means the beach is narrower than the height of the cliff, I go a different way. In company, I might take more risks with the elements, because I might be rescued, but even so, I think about each situation as an individual, not one of a herd.

As I finished writing this book and naturally returned to the beginning, a full-moon storm had just exposed the sea defences on the beach below us. When we first arrived, these concrete pyramids were at the foot of the cliff, but now they are many metres away on the beach, or more usually under the beach, measuring our ebbing time with invisibly brutal accuracy. By eye, it is clear that the distance from the sea defences to the bottom of the cliff is now twice the distance from the cliff edge to the house itself. The two-thirds on the beach equal the ten years we have been here, so the one-third on the clifftop implies that we might still have five years. Two-thirds of our time here seem to have just vanished into thin air yet I find the literal, visible erosion of time to be oddly comforting.

The last defined purpose of this place was in the war, looking outwards not inwards, scanning the world beyond. A new planning application proposes to knock down the farm building which then served as the radar station. By chance, a photograph I took of that building ended up as the winner of the inaugural 'Suffolk Beauty' photography competition, so it is recorded for posterity. Little did I know how prematurely that significant little landmark would be destroyed, and by forces other than the erosion.

The Easternmost House is a portrait of a place that soon will no longer exist. It is a memorial to this house and the lost village it represents, and to our ephemeral life here, so that something of it will remain once it has all gone.

> At the beach, life is different. Time doesn't move hour to hour, but mood to moment.
> We live by the currents, plan by the tides, and follow the sun.
>
> *Anon/Unknown*

The Beach and the Cliff

I have desired to go
Where the springs not fail,
To fields where flies no sharp and sided hail
And few lilies blow.
Where no storms come,
Where the green swell is in the havens dumb,
And out of the swing of the sea.

Heaven-Haven
Gerard Manley Hopkins (1844-1889)

1
JANUARY

Genius Loci, A Sense Of Place

East of London, east of Ipswich and east of all the rest of England, there sits upon a cliff this little house, this remote house from whose kitchen table I try to convey the spirit and beauty of the place to others. It is a wind-blown house on the edge of an eroding clifftop at the easternmost end of a track which leads only into the sea. The farm track looks as if it wants to continue for a mile or two, but it has been hacked off roughly by the wind and sea and erosion. There used to be a village here and there used to be several hundred more acres of farmland. This farm used to own the easternmost land mass in the whole of Britain, and the little village used to be at the heart of the easternmost parish: Easton Bavents.

The word 'east' appears three times in our Easton Bavents address, four if you add Easton Farm and five if you count the fact that we are in East Anglia. There is much here that 'used to be', and it seems sad and unro-mantic that the actual easternmost point of Britain is now an uncelebrated spot in Lowestoft. Soon, the house we live in will be described as the house that 'used to be' right on the edge. The jagged edge is always a warning, of recent erosion, of unknown cliff conditions underfoot, of new chunks of land having fallen into the sea overnight.

The church of St. Nicholas Easton Bavents used to be the easternmost church in England, and it was the presence of the church that made Easton Bavents the easternmost parish. The easternmost land mass stuck out into the sea like a nose, marked on old maps as Easton Ness. The last known vicar here was appointed in 1666, and a storm soon after that destroyed the church. The church of St. Nicholas is now a mile and a half out to sea, further east than the more famous vanished churches of the 'lost city' of Dunwich, and without the mythical bells supposedly ringing on stormy nights. The role of churchwarden here is mercifully light on duties, reduced only to a ghostly sense of responsibility to keep the memory of the easternmost church alive.

Within sight from the house and the cliff is a distant postcard view of Southwold, but the cliff is a wild place, bashed about by raw nature. In summer it is like living in a Mediterranean paradise. In winter it can be like living on a wind-lashed trawler. The Suffolk coast is eerie and deceptive like that. This watery landscape looks pretty but it conceals many ways to cast tragedy over the unwary or the over-confident on their summer holidays. The photogenic harbour with its picture-book boats hides its racing tides. The sun-blessed reedbeds hide their disorientating scale and dangerously invisible water-filled dykes. The clifftop path through casual drifts of wild flowers hides lethal cantilevered ledges of sand, unsupported land, hovering over thin air, preparing imminently to crash onto the beach below. Land, sea and sky are unheeding of the line in the hymn, 'its own appointed limits keep'. Here, the 'mighty ocean deep' keeps to no appointed limits.

You can see the house from a long way off if you know where to look. From particular viewpoints, its tiny form is glimpsed on the ridge beyond the reedbeds, sheltering under the wide skies in the distance just to the left of the pepperpot white lighthouse. A line of Scots Pines on another ridge forms the sort of treescape familiar to Pooh and Piglet and Eeyore. Driving along the road about a mile away, you sense but cannot see that the land is about to run out, and the little house stands firm against painterly swoops of light and colour and cloud, in a place where it is never quite clear which is land and which is sea or sky. The house is invisible to all but those who know intimately how it is placed in the lie of the land. Alone, away from the herd, it is only from afar that you really appreciate how tiny this house seems against the vastness of nature's uncaring dramas and our wide East Anglian skies. From the sea, it appears as a house from an old-fashioned story book.

Imagine you are approaching the house. You could walk past the pier and the beach huts in Southwold and continue north to where there is a sign saying PRIVATE EASTON BAVENTS (perhaps a subordinate of General

Principle) and just keep going. By car, you would turn off a winding rural road, into a long farm track with a sign warning of SLOW CHILDREN AND ANIMALS and follow the telegraph poles all the way to the end. However you achieve it, you need to be alert once you arrive, because this is the edge of the cliff, and before you now, only a small sign decorated with a skull and crossbones and the message DANGER CLIFF ERODING, then a vertical drop and the sea.

The views from the danger-cliff are friendly. To the north there is an uncluttered view of open arable land and the beach towards Benacre, pronounced BENakker, not Ben Acre like a character from *The Archers*. To the south, there are more crops and beyond that, Southwold: pier, lighthouse, brewery, church, water tower. The cliff hides lines and layers of history beneath your feet, but from the beach, the layers are made visible by the erosion, telling part of the story of millions of years of time and our place in it: about 60 million years since the birds evolved, 10 million years since the first humans, two million years'-worth of tiny animals now exposed to our eyes in the cliff, and about 6000 years since this piece of land was walkable from mainland Europe, via Doggerland.

It is odd to think how our ancient ancestors would have experienced exactly the same great rhythms of sea and tide and wind, and the same silence. The sound of the sea crashing on the beach must be deeply embedded into our collective race memory. Will future geologists look askance at the damage wrought by only fifty years of plastic? Will those plastic islands in the Pacific that we read about in despair become layered with airborne earth and guano and seeds and renewal and eventually become real islands lush with their own natural beauty?

To the practical and business-like eye, we are surrounded by 'resources'. There is several hundred years'-worth of thatched roofing hidden in the reedbeds. Along the clifftop, every tuft of these primitive grasses is a relation of those which led us to cultivate wheat and barley, the crops on the clifftop now, divided by a straight furrow from the rough path and the jagged grassy cliff edge. The plough and tractor tramlines often appear to drive straight off the edge, as the lines and angles drawn by agricultural machinery change every year according to the ever-changing boundary. The gourmand should sense the perpetual proximity of wild fish and game, in fur, feather, fin and shell. Within our immediate view, a free-range bacon sandwich and pint of beer are the crops, all the necessary ingredients grown within one food-mile of the house, and Colman's English Mustard is just up the road in Norfolk. To the poet-adventurer, every wild flower carries folkloric or medicinal meaning. Among the fluttering sea of red on the clifftop, each little poppy shrugging off the salt-spray is a small miracle of resilience and survival.

Wild animals and birds come and go with the seasons: the graceful, the comical, the rare, the beautiful and the noisy, sometimes as familiar as pets and at other times utterly mysterious and elusive. The resident barn owl and fox and the semi-tame pheasant, can surely not possibly be literally the same individuals after so many years. They must be like the Andrex puppy or the Dulux dog, or the perpetual supply of soldiers in bearskins marching about in London, *multi juncta in uno*, to paraphrase the motto of the Household Division, many joined in one to offer a reassuring sense of continuity and immortality.

A quiet whipping sound in the air can suddenly give way to vast V-formations of quietly honking geese drifting across our skies, their ragged skeins stretching out over the sea as they home in on favourite feeding grounds, crowding in behind the house with the contented murmur of their voices as they graze on the late stubbles. Terns and gulls wheel and cry over the beach, empty and deserted of all human life. Most of the time, apart from the companionable chatter of birds against the sounds of the sea, there is total silence.

Otters visit their own private pooling place and friendly dog-like fat seals sometimes bask in the sun on the beach under the house at particular times of year. Otters have occasionally been seen at a place marked on the map as Potters Bridge, which I like to think might be a corruption of an older name, Otters' Bridge. On summer evenings, the song of invisible crickets fills the air, and the cliff-edge wildflower drifts become abuzz with every sort of flying of mini-creature. At dusk, the stripey feral cliff-cat comes out of hiding to prowl around its own secret domain, avoiding the fox, needless of people.

These beach-based and cliff-top creatures mix and overlap with a mingling miscellany of permanent people and passers-by to create a convivial succession of natural events and incidents, small coastal crises, everyday disasters and adventures, all year round. And always, in our little patch of this earthly paradise, there will be a greyhound porpoising about you, not far away, covering the ground with a graceful wave movement.

With this little book as your pocket-cottage, you can tramp on our wide flat sands and scrunch over the banks of shingle on the beach, with the imaginary cold salt-wind in your face. Look at the night sky, consider the moon, feel the distant stars filling in the deep dark sky between the brightest dots with the cloudy infinity of the milky way, as your eyes adjust to the unimaginable billions of their numbers and light-years and times and distances and sizes.

The physical extremity of this location serves to enhance the sense of destination, and of arrival. As you make your imaginary turn into the farm track (rough gravel with grass up the middle) and head up the track towards the end, suddenly you see it: the house and then the sea. To come to the real-life Easternmost House is to enter another world, a foreign country, the past, a very real sense of what the writers of *The Book of Common Prayer* meant by 'that peace which the world cannot give', a phrase written at about the time our church fell into the sea.

You will not find the church of St. Nicholas, Easton Bavents, in your Pevsner guide to the buildings of Suffolk, nor will you feel guilty when you repeatedly fail to be present in your pew as a regular member of the congregation, for you have the perfect excuse for missing matins on a Sunday morning: you are not a fish. As our parish church sits quietly on the seabed, part buried here, recognisable pieces of architecture there, perhaps a little buttress among the silvery bass swimming around the ruins beneath the waves, the memory of its existence adds to the sense of calm.

Living in a place where the church fell into the sea three hundred years ago makes it quite easy to imagine life in the future: not just a decade hence, but fifty years, a century, or three centuries hence. What will be exactly here, at X? What will the world be like? Will any people have landed on Mars? Will we have invented our way out of plastic, poverty, famine? There was only ever a small fishing village up on this cliff and it has always been a shifting land of shingle and sand. Here, the history of houses and farmland being lost to the sea reaches far away back into time, a known unknown.

The erosion process is historic and ongoing, with years of stability followed by great crashes of land-loss in a single tide. As the cliff face is worn away, fossils are exposed, theoretically presenting centuries of the purest Pleistocene-era archaeological trench, ready-prepared for fossil-hunters to study. Tiny creatures who have not seen the sun for millions of years are suddenly revealed. It is a little disappointing not to unearth a whole proper dinosaur, or giant squid, or at least a recognisable fish, but there is a quiet thrill in accidentally stumbling upon any part of an ancient animal, however simple the life-form, and to hold in your hand a little stripey stone that was a maggot-like-creature perhaps two million years ago.

Within the unremarkable stones on the beach can be found some small wonders of life and there have been a few whole mammoth bones found in our cliff, allegedly 600,000 years old. When this landscape was physically connected to mainland Europe, at auspicious times of year people could walk all the way overland, over what is now the North Sea, in search of the good mammoth-hunting opportunities which must have presented themselves in and around Southwold. At its deepest, the North Sea is apparently still only one Nelson's Column deep.

Sometimes the erosion makes the national news. Some of our more dramatic cliff-edge demolitions or land-falls have appeared on television and in newspapers. More frequently we feature on the local news. An aerial photograph showing the Easternmost House, looking tiny on the cliff edge, was on a front page not long ago, with a similar photograph taken a year earlier to illustrate the extent of recent erosion, the whole ensemble captioned, ALARMING.

The extent of our natural territory is loosely defined by the foot-radius of local walking distance and boat-radius on the sea. Our kind of walking is free of the paraphernalia and intense ambitions of the hard-pushing hiker or the rose-tinted rambler. We walk quite far, quite often, but always with some greater purpose, and with Chuffy the Brindle Bomber Greyhound, so that the walking itself is incidental to the reason for it: the foraging for firewood, the seeking out of seeds, the scavenging of marsh samphire or the perpetual quest of the beachcomber.

In the manner of all good treasure maps, as well as being edged by natural boundaries of reedbeds, river and sea, our territory also contains distinct zones and landmarks. One of these is a peculiar natural sculpture gallery. On a far ridge to the north, the farm adjoins the estate it used to belong to at Benacre, before the farm was sold to pay for death duties in the 1920s, and it is on this boundary of our territory that some unremarkable pines lead to a spooky place where the cliff tumbles down into what appears to be a prehistoric forest but can't be. Here, there are white-boned fossilised trees on the beach, a bleached-out stumpery, trunks and branches emerge half-buried from the sand in artful compositions and sculptural groupings. There used to be a single, special tree, standing up on the beach, with branches formed like giant but gentle fingers, the Benacre Tree. One sad day, the Benacre Tree had gone. These strange trees are also reflected in the water of the broad, a lake behind the beach, where water and fossil-trees, and sunsets, and reflections of everything mingle on both sides, making a disorientating experience.

There is a particularly white-smooth fossil-tree with ZEUS inscribed into its half-buried bone-like trunk, in a perfectly formed Roman font about two inches high, with fine serifs, as if carved yesterday afternoon by some passing Roman invader with a fetish for advanced letter-cutting. The Zeus Tree is an ideal place of contemplation, a reading and writing tree, a sketching tree, warmed by white-hot glaring sands under summer suns, but sheltering against the worst of the salt-winds in rougher seasons, a kind tree, a destination, an old friend.

The reedbeds conceal the misty, marshy homes of mysterious wild creatures seldom seen and is the source of many haunting sounds. Nearby is the place where the swans meet and the otters come for their pooling pleasures. The bittern booms. To reveal too much about the precise habits and locations of our wild companions would be to betray their secrets, bringing nearer their enemies of camera lens and 'sharing'. A single tweet could bring an invading army of long lenses.

To the south of our treasure map, our territory ends with the River Blyth with Walberswick on the far side. Southwold Harbour outposts of the Easternmost House are a tarred-timber boat hut, a fast inflatable orange boat and its landing stage, a hut selling fish caught from a boat moored opposite, and the Harbour Inn, from which one is bound to watch the sunsets, as coastal peoples always have and always will. The wetland circle is completed by the Blyth Estuary as it opens out into a wide expanse of water hiding local secrets of navigable routes and shallows, marked out with timber posts to offer a miniature vision of the Venetian lagoon as it might have looked when the early Venetians began trading, or an unexpected insight into the homelands of the Marsh Arabs of Iraq.

Returning to the Easternmost House from the far beach near the Zeus Tree, the house appears as a tiny dark rectangle in an enormous skyscape, like a little matchbox placed on the mantelpiece in front of one of the larger of Turner's most abstracted weather-inspired canvasses, sometimes all dark blues and steely greys, sometimes the wildest fires of unnaturally loud pinks and oranges, dazzling vast and bright and all-encompassing. Exaggerated highlights and powder-puff pink clouds at sunset could part to reveal a flight of Renaissance *putti* at any moment. At dusk or in the dark, eerie glowing effects from the distant lighthouse reach far down the beach. This landscape is one of ever-changing readjustment, undefined by the spectacle or the solidity of rock or mountain, but there is no excuse to call it dull and flat, and not to see that to be outside under these wide skies is to feel closer to something that the modern world has almost lost.

The odd little world of Easton Bavents is connected to the rest of the world by the A12, a road which may one day become a causeway when the Blyth Estuary will have expanded and the inland River Blyth will have become wide water all the way along the valley. To north, west and south we are ringed by reedbed and river. To the east, there is only the sea. We are practically an island. Despite or because of the impending sense of separateness and impermanence, there is so much quiet beauty in this landscape of light and sky that those who find it, find they cannot leave.

JANUARY

Food in season and local 'sea state' update

Veg
Beetroot, cabbage, spinach, chard, onions, potatoes

Fruit
Seville oranges and the marmalade-making season

Game
Pheasant, partridge, mallard, pigeon, rabbit, hare

Fish
Brill, cod, flounder, John Dory, scallops

Distance from cliff
24 metres, measured to front/seaward corner of house,
but not a precise science

Change since last month
Cliff loss approx. 500mm, loss of part of hedge at edge

Music in its Roar

There is a pleasure in the pathless woods,
There is a rapture on the lonely shore,
There is society, where none intrudes,
By the deep sea, and music in its roar;
I love not man the less, but Nature more.

Childe Harold's Pilgrimage
George Gordon, Lord Byron (1788-1824)

2

FEBRUARY

February brings tidal surges and moody contrasts, but also the first signs of spring. Some of the worst losses of cliff have been at this time of year. 'Beast from the East' winds and snowstorms can be followed the next day by blue skies, bright sunshine and emerging snowdrops. Sharp shadows and light combinations make photography safaris tempting and rewarding of the effort. A storm of Twitter trends, #Snowmaggeddon, #Friday13th and #TidalSurge, are simultaneously gathered in the same place, here, on one afternoon. Horizontal windy snow made it a matter of active concentration to be sensible, to not be the naive idiot blown off the edge of the cliff. Iron grey skies and white drifts of snow on the beach looked like a painting, not real life.

With the evenings still dark and the fires still burning, inevitably less time is spent outside, more hunkering down to 'indoor jobs' at the clifftop kitchen table. This might be a good moment to convey a little of the house itself and explain how we earn a living, and how we came to be here.

I am a qualified architect, but I have also been paid to tend vines, ride horses, wrangle sheep, roll fleeces, drive a boat, write, draw, prune, paint-and-decorate, and generally be useful and versatile. For several years, I contributed cartoons to architecture magazines, including the Prince of Wales's pet project at the time and some of these were shown at the Royal Academy Summer Exhibition.

I first discovered how to access the private farm at Easton Bavents when I was paid to do some drawings up here, about fifteen years ago. I chose architecture partly because I grew up surrounded by beautiful old buildings and thought it would be a useful set of skills to have. I also grew up surrounded by animals, so in another life I might equally have chosen to become a vet, for the same reason. I perhaps didn't appreciate the steepness of learning curve when I embarked on this mission, but I now have a working knowledge of both Brutalism and bloodstock (the breeding of racehorses), worlds apart, united only by the often untrue architectural aphorism, 'form follows function'. My husband, Giles, is a career soldier, an officer in the Household Cavalry and now runs the Household Cavalry Foundation, their regimental charity, based at Horse Guards but often working from the clifftop kitchen table. We have known each other since our early prime.

We rent the Easternmost House from Easton Farm, the farm on which it sits, so the financial loss of the erosion is to the farm, in lost rent, lost land and lost crops. Easton Farm was part of a large estate, Benacre, this farm being sold off to pay death duties in the 1920s. The wider context of our coastal home territory includes everything within a radius reaching from the sea, up the river Blyth estuary, and approximately out to the rambling old rectory which was my childhood home (known locally by everyone as the 'Old Rec'). Beyond that, it no longer counts as home territory.

Despite spending many years away, having grown up here and taken for granted its casual beauty as a child, I know the landscape in ways that can't be seen just by looking at it. This is where the fire got out of control, this is where we saw a dead fox on a straw stack, this is the field where the donkeys used to live, those are the hedges we used to jump, Sternacre Farm used to be called Stark Naked Farm, and so on. There are many people I have known since childhood, a mixed bag of landowners, farmers, fishermen, farriers, gamekeepers, friends and even one or two foes. I also know who owns most of the landscape around me and where the boundaries are. So I feel rooted here, as hefted to my place as a sheep might be to the Fells or Dales.

Driving through the landscape as a visitor, Suffolk farmland may look like a 'wildlife desert', as TV conservationists claim the entire British landscape to be, but at dusk I could take you to places where I guarantee you would see at least ten hares and five barn owls on any typical evening and at dawn, the sky is alive with the sound of skylarks. The raucous dawn chorus is Suffolk's cosy impersonation of a rainforest, but the sound is a positive indication of bird life that would not be evident in a picture, or if you were not here at dawn. Our 'rainforest' was never much more dramatic than the remaining gorse-scrub and heathland known as the sandlings, tamed by our ancestors long ago. There is a constant buzzing of insects in the 'rough'. Rachel Carson, who wrote the famously depressing but important book, *Silent Spring*, would be encouraged.

These are some bald explanatory background facts, of the sort that I always want to know when reading, say, a book about someone living a magical life in a sun-drenched stone farmhouse in Liguria. Where does the money come from? What do they do when not telling me about their sun-kissed olive groves and bountiful tomato and basil crops? Where do they buy coffee and loo paper? Does it ever rain? How did they come to be there at all? Are they alone? Et cetera.

The house itself was originally a row of three Benacre estate cottages, built for farm labourers or similar, difficult to date, but probably about 1800. Practical, solid, honest and well-proportioned, with fireplaces and original features intact, but also a bit butchered by 'improvements' over the years. It is red brick, with dark pantiles, referred to in Suffolk as 'blue' pantiles, but actually a dark grey-black, and very typical of the local vernacular. The wall facing the sea is painted pink, also very typically Suffolk. It has its original bead-and-butt doors with Suffolk latches, and the old threshold timbers are worn into soft curves by the boots of farm labourers past, hinting that it might be older than it at first looks. The defining feature of the house, that makes it recognisable from afar across the fields and trees, or from some distant part of the beach, is its chimneys. Because of being originally three cottages, with two being mirror-images of each other in plan, plus the one nearest the cliff-edge, the chimney line goes: chimney, space, space, chimney, space, chimney.

Something like this: I____I__I

With regard to its contents, a specific item of beach flotsam acts as an unlikely but relevant prompt.

A bright orange buoy was washed up on the beach below our cliff one morning, to herald the dawn of Valentine's Day, a date which in Suffolk is significant as the start of the new racehorse-breeding season in Newmarket over yonder at the other side of the county (eleven months gestation and the January 1st racehorse birthday making it a safe date to avoid a late December foal, who could be 'one year old' when in fact only one week old). For obvious reasons relating to its size and colour, the orange buoy prompted me to be haunted by the Spectre of the Space Hopper, the spectre of impending poverty and disaster which haunted my childhood. I asked Giles whether he knew what I meant by a space hopper. 'It's one of those orange blobs with ears that everybody bounced around on as children.' Exactly. It's one of those orange blobs *with ears* that everybody *else* bounced around on as children.

My disproportionate childhood expectation of real and imminent poverty can be traced to The Affair of the

Space Hopper and its wider cultural context, which goes like this:

Once upon a time, I wanted a space hopper more than anything in the whole world, and shyly hinted about it before every likely present-receiving opportunity, to no avail. Eventually, I resigned myself to the familiar conclusion that the parental consensus was either that it was a waste of money because we could improvise something similar for nothing, or that a space hopper was a passing fad that had no use or value *in the long term*. Instead, I was given old things, such as a silver hand-held mirror, or Granny's childhood hunting whip, with a whalebone gate-opening hook at one end and a plaited leather lash at the other and my initials engraved on its small silver band. The parental consensus was wise, as I still have the various 'old things' given to me instead of a space hopper. I am eternally grateful for those beautiful old things now, but I was understandably less enchanted when I was about seven years old and my heart desired a space hopper.

So, back to the new orange buoy on the beach and how this is relevant to anything about the Easternmost House itself. In the inevitable absence of a real space hopper, my ex-army father made a space hopper substitute from a similar deflated old buoy we had found on the beach all those years ago, patched with squares of black gaffer tape. It had a bit of rope to hold on to and it had a certain battered beach-life chic about it, but as a space hopper it was absolutely hopeless. It didn't bounce properly, being half deflated all the time, and it was heavy. Nor did it have the silly grinning face, with a little topknot above the squinting eyes. But its main and most unforgivable failure as a proper space hopper was its lack of the ribbed ears that define the object. The only part of its space hopper impersonation that it pulled off with any aplomb was the colour. It was predominantly orange, but even in that it failed because it had a big black plimsoll-line end.

I pretended it was far cooler than the real thing, but it set a seed of insecurity, that our parents and Granny could only afford to give us 'old things', rather than choosing to for reasons of not valuing space hoppers. After its reincarnation as a space hopper, the original orange buoy enjoyed a third career. Cut in half, the hemispherical half (as distinct from the more pointy top) became a mould for the production of home-made concrete balls to set on two stumpy brick pillars framing some garden steps at the Old Rec, concrete-ball-making being a dotage pastime of my late father, along with building flint walls, in the manner of the famous bricklayer, Winston Churchill. The point about the space-hopper-improvising episode is that it was absolutely normal, for us.

A curious aspect of my childhood was the complete absence of modernity about it, even though it was the 1970s. The oldness of the objects around us was not just confined to the big, obvious things, like the house, furniture and pictures, but to small, everyday items as well. From the moment we were plonked in the big black coach-sprung pram, our relationship with this 'old stuff' began. We ate with old knives and forks, off old plates (with the salt in a little heap on the side of the plate), wearing handed-down clothes, before saying, 'Please may I get down?' We read old copies of old books: *Struwwelpeter, Vermilion, The Fox's Frolic, Little Black Sambo* and *The House at Pooh Corner*, and a long line of all those little ones by Beatrix Potter.

We had baths in an old bath, with threadbare old bath mats. Even the soap seemed to smell of 'oldness'. There was an old, slightly rusty metal poem: 'Please remember, don't forget! Never leave the bathroom wet'. We went to bed in old beds, with old sheets, old blankets, old pillows, and old eiderdowns with the feathers falling out. And we still do, because the Easternmost House is furnished with a distillation of these same 'old things', it being filled with all the 'old things' that other members of our families didn't want. The house itself is a refugee from a larger estate and most of the contents are similarly refugees from a past life larger than ours is now.

A memorable 'old things' toy at the Old Rec was a collection of Britain's model hunting people on horses, some headless, legless, armless and/or chipped, but complete with a pack of hounds and a very fleet-of-foot-looking fox. The whole hunting ensemble was made of solid lead and carefully hand-painted with lead paint. The lead hunting collection had small parts to choke on, was politically incorrect in subject matter, and was (is) entirely toxic. The toxic hunting scene now resides at the Easternmost House, where it looks odd galloping along a window sill, with the sea raging enormously behind it. But this historical context goes some way to explain why the Easternmost House is entirely furnished with other people's cast-offs. It also illustrates the degree to which none of us has much choice in the influences which define our formative early years.

As children, we were feral, outdoors and unsupervised most of the time, sent to boarding school seven counties away, sent out hunting for character-building purposes in the relevant holidays and generally indoctrinated with old-school values, using all our old things in normal everyday life. Until one day we were suddenly all grown-up, and emerged blinking from our proto-nineteenth-century upbringings into the last throes of the twentieth century. And then the twenty-first century. Back to the clifftop here and now.

Paradoxically, our 'old stuff' is typical of the British system of one-downmanship, which now translates into eco-friendliness. 'Old stuff'-users could never be considered wasteful or *nouveau riche*. Nor any other kind of *riche* as it happened. When we were children, I watched in horror as a favourite uncle decided that family HQ, a crumbling estate in Berkshire called Adbury Park, where my mother's family had lived for generations, was a white elephant that would at some stage be gobbled up with home counties development and should be exchanged for an efficient farm in Norfolk, so he sold it to a man who had made a fortune in butter. The butter king demolished everything, except the stable yard, the kitchen garden and Granny, who refused to leave her cottage. Granny remained there, overlooking the park, defiantly pouring her milk from her *Eton Boating Song* musical jug and reading *The Sport of our Ancestors,* to the bitter end. In the barbarian 1970s, such architectural vandalism was all the rage. The demolition of England's country houses by the Philistines was commonplace. It was worse than the loss of a house to coastal erosion could ever be.

The mere sight of the orange buoy which washed up on the beach on Valentine's Day had much the same effect on me as the madeleine had on Proust, prompting remembrance of home-made and old things past, the buoy space hopper and its associations leading seamlessly into memories of the demolition of that beautiful old country house by the wrecking ball. When the wrecking ball and the yellow digger comes for our house on the cliff, I will have been there before. It will be strange seeing into the half-demolished rooms where we have been so happy, but I think it will also be compulsive watching, not something to avoid or for which to be absent.

From the lofty vantage point of the clifftop, hindsight and the present day, I can see that having only a home-made space hopper was a character-building privilege, and that the memorable old orange buoy belongs to the England of sunlit uplands and daisies on lawns, Ladybird Books and P. G. Wodehouse, plimsolls and wooden tennis rackets, in a way that a real one probably never could. Inevitably, I litter-pick the new orange buoy off the beach, and take it home as a treasure

Sounds and Storms

The slow sound of creaking timber, the groans of enforced stress, must have been familiar and terrifying to our ancestors, especially to the pioneering architects and builders of the past, attempting large experimental structures. These noises are the harbingers of shipwreck and imminent structural failure.

The Shipping Forecast warned of gales in every sea area, but the night-clankings outside and the wind moaning down the chimney, told us all we needed to know about the weather in North Utsire. The sea has many different sounds, but that night it was the full churning roar. The winds of a thousand miles buffeted and blew, wind over tide, wave over beach, the whole force of accumulated energy finally crashing up against our cliff. From an upper seaward window, it appeared as if the sea was churning right up to the top. The beautiful archaic language which speaks of the 'foaming deep' and 'mighty works' seems entirely apt and contemporary up here. Ordinary quiet sounds, of the dog snoring and rain on the roof, are comfortingly discernible against a roaring storm, just as tiny tweety birdsong is audible in Hyde Park, against the growling grey roar of the traffic.

In the eerie calm of the aftermath of the storm, our interest was piqued by reports of a cargo ship beginning to break up in the English Channel, with the anticipated loss of its cargo. While those in peril out at sea kept watch for the unknown hazards afloat, the foraging instincts of an island race had been stirred and awakened on the shore. All along the coast of sea areas Dover, Wight and

Portland, sea people started to look out for the unspeci-fied cargo washing up on their beaches. This must have always happened from time to time, creating unfamiliar situations where real life and folklore seem to blur in the collective memory. From Whisky Galore on Eriskay to the Great BMW Motorbike Rush of Dorset, the heart of the primitive wrecker still beats in us all.

As an abstract idea, salvage from a wreck is a romantic notion, out of a stable not too far away from pillage, poaching and piracy, and with the same potential for raffish roguishness or brutal criminality. It is buried deep in our race memory and shipwreck timbers are buried deep in the structures of our coastal houses and pubs. On a local level, it is just exaggerated beachcombing: the resourceful use of available materials; a noble con-tinuity of centuries of improvisation and initiative; the antithesis of modern consumerism and wastefulness. Yet regardless of the nature of the goods on board the ship, a real-life shipwreck poses unexpected moral dilemmas.

Although supposedly due to be washed up on the south coast, the prospect of an imminent shipwreck on our shore stirred up east coast wrecking memories. One is suddenly transported with some clarity back to the earliest stages in the evolution of civilised societies and of our legal systems and our moral mazes. When does salvage become stealing? When does stealing become looting? Which is worse? Looting, because it is taking more than one needs? Is it unacceptable to take more than one needs? No? Even if useful and valuable things will be lost to the incoming tide? Isn't it a waste of our finite natural resources to just leave them there? And anyway, doesn't spilt cargo become the most frightful case of litter, which we have an urgent duty to clear up? Who does stuff belong to once it is in the sea? Or on the beach?

How do people co-operate in the salvage operation to maximise mutual benefit? How do they share the fruits of efforts, if at all? Is it pigs in the trough, survival of the fittest, winner takes all, or are we more civilised now? These moral grey areas must have preyed on human minds since the first man stood up and opposed his thumb against his finger to nick a few of his dozing neighbour's cobnuts. We pondered briefly on the moral philosophy of salvage and kept an eye out for unusual bounty on the beach, but none came.

A common sound of life on a windblown cliff is that of hammering nails into timber after gales. Repairs. After one such hurricane, I was greeted the next morning by the sight of a tree, decorated in its upper branches with neat strips of undamaged corrugated iron. This was the roof of the shed that the chickens roost in. Their door was wide open to the foxes, for the door too had found its way into the tree. I braced myself for the inevitable carnage, or for a search for the bodies of my little terrified friends. The sting of sadness which accompanies the death of any animal, and especially any animal in my care, began to prick my conscience.

Then two little hen-faces appeared at the open doorway, standing resolutely just inside their house, not daring to venture outside. Then they began to cluck in what anyone but a scientist would say was an overwhelming chorus of chicken-happiness and genuine relief, to see me, and to feel safe again. Cockle was still on his perch. My theory is that Chuffy the Brindle Greyhound marks our territory with a fox-warning, fox-proofing scent. Instead of the sting of mourning our chickens, it was a morning of tree-laddering and roof-hammering, practising the skills that guests on *Desert Island Discs* are so often asked if they possess. Usually people claim not to be able to build themselves a hut or skin a rabbit, but it may yet prove unwise not to hone these essential survival skills, especially where shelter and food are concerned, in case we might need them again, *in extremis*. In case nature one day might bite us back.

The sounds of our territory range from the noisy crashing of waves and wind, to the tiniest quiet chirrups and the long summer of assorted buzzings. Some the most mysterious sounds emanate from the reedbeds. The cry of the curlew from the grass-tops of the cliff could stir the soul of any red-blooded poet-adventurer, but the boom of the bittern in the reeds is the most arresting and characteristic sound of this place.

To hear the boom of the bittern, you could retire to one of the quieter places of contemplation, perhaps to the Zeus Tree, beside the nearest of the brackish broads, the marshy pools behind the beach. There, you could contemplate the grace and mutual affection of the swans, who apparently have the endearing habit of becoming anxious if they can't see their family all together at the same time. You could wait on the off-chance for a mischievous appearance of the otters. You will certainly be giddied by the wheeling of the assorted gulls and terns, sea-swallows, and in summer you may find a friendly seal for your dog-like companionable needs.

With these watchings, you will be always entertained. It is a good excuse to stop and stare. Wild creatures generally prefer you to be still if you wish to observe them doing anything interesting or hear them boom. You will have time to wonder who carved the small but perfect ZEUS, in capital letters, into the bleached trunk of the Zeus Tree, and why, and whether or not it is art or vandalism. Zeus, the master of disguise with the morals of a dog, who appears as a swan in a Venetian painting by Titian, now appears artfully on a tree on the private shore of our salty coastal lake, Easton Broad, where the swans gather and mate for life.

Nature-spotting books will tell you that you are most likely to hear the boom of the bittern in spring, in the early morning at sunrise, or in the evening, and that the number of booms heard together should reduce from about six to about two as summer progresses. Here, in real life, I think you may hear a single boom or several, at any time of the day, at any time of the year, and even when talking and walking with dogs. It is a haunting sound, a sound that hints of spookiness and rarity, like a very low-pitched foghorn, or someone blowing quite suddenly and strongly over the rim of an empty bottle. Apparently, the low pitch of the sounds means that it carried for three miles, to a receptive other bittern. Whoooumph. Whoooumph. That rare bottle-blown sound is the boom of the bittern in the reedbeds nearby and you will feel a privileged person to have heard it.

Susurration. Susurrus. Sibilance. Sibilant. Phloisbos.

These are some of our English words for 'the sound of waves on a shingle beach'. Listening on the beach, it becomes evident that their true meaning is more complex, something more like, 'the combined total sound of the waves approaching, breaking and then retreating on a shingle beach', and/or the verb relating to making that sound. There are combinations of crashes and splashes, and sometimes almost cracks of gunfire or the low-frequency boom of a bomb from which you can feel vibrations through the ground under your feet, followed by assorted extended families of foamings and shushings, sometimes with little whistlings.

Our English teachers might once have told us that onomatopoeia is the formation of words from sound associated with the thing named: cuckoo, sizzle, ping, etc., encouraging us to think how effective this idea is in conveying sounds in general. The concept of susurration illustrates the limitations of English, and teachers, and of even the most onomatopoeic words to convey sounds convincingly at all. Even though the entire combination of all these conceptual words is instantly recognisable as a single sound, it is practically impossible to write down, unless perhaps you try and use a musical score. For as long as there have been humans, and as long as there will be humans, the sound of waves over a shingle beach has been known to them. It is the perpetual background sound of this place and with it from time to time comes a piece of living history, washed up on the next tide.

A piece of wood with circular holes and pegs in it turned out to be part of an eighteenth-century ship. A piece of stone turned out to be engraved with part of a name, probably from someone's grave in the churchyard at Covehithe, a mile or two north of our beach, near the place which lost sixteen metres of land in one tide. Every pebble on this beach is its own little world of mineral and memory, hiding unknown secrets from thousands of years ago. And onto this little beach from time to time, the combined great oceans of the world fling unexpected gifts of flotsam and jetsam and random bounty.

The sounds of danger ought to be embedded in our instincts, but sometimes our clever inventions drown them out. Witness the chainsaw. Just as the creaking of timber must have alerted our ancestors to impending structural collapse, so the sound of the chainsaw should immediately stiffen the sinews and raise the hackles of even the most urban and urbane sophisticate. It is a harbinger of impending destruction, laden with potential dangers.

In the wider territory of the Easternmost House is my childhood home, where a large tree fell down in a storm. There are many competent people wielding chainsaws and in possession of suitable formal qualifications and licences. But not all chainsaw-wielders are tree surgeons and fallen trees can behave unexpectedly. Some years ago, a gang of local chainsaw enthusiasts, or at least a few people who lived within a radius of the tree in question and owned a chainsaw, set about chopping it up. It could not be left where it fell, to become an 'eco-system', because it would interfere with the annual cricket-pitch arrangements. So the chainsaw enthusiasts began to chop it up, as they had many other such trees, starting with the branches. The five or so roaring amateur chainsaw-ists made light work of the outer branches, later to become useful logs, so they then set about the larger branches nearer the trunk. There probably was a sound, some sound that our ancestors would have recognised as a warning, some creaking such as might be heard in the beams of a pirate ship. But roars and growls of the chainsaws would have drowned it out, even if it had been audible to the modern 'naked ear'.

The tree defied its fate and moved slightly, almost imperceptibly and then it mysteriously rose from the dead and stood straight back up, its balance somehow restored to the point of equilibrium with its roots. By the end of the chainsaw session, far from being chopped into transportable, saleable timber and logs, the tree was standing proudly back where it had always stood, just with the odd attentions of non-tree-surgeons having ruined its branches.

The chainsaw gang were uncharacteristically jocular about the incident afterwards, which was proof enough that the tree-ghost had given them all a terrible fright.

FEBRUARY

Food in season and local 'sea state' update

Veg
Brussels sprouts, salsify, shallots, kale, sprouting broccoli

Fruit
Seville oranges, last chance for home-made marmalade
Rhubarb

Game
Wild duck, rabbit, hare

Fish
Lemon sole and other flatfish, wild salmon season begins

Distance from cliff
22 metres

Change since last month
2 metres cliff loss, loss of small tree a noticeable
visual difference

The Timber Tide

Glory be to God for dappled things,
For skies of couple-colour as a brinded cow;
For rose-moles all in stipple upon trout that swim;
Landscape plotted and pieced – fold, fallow and plough;
And all trades, their gear and tackle and trim

Pied Beauty
Gerard Manley Hopkins (1844-1889)

3

MARCH

It is difficult not to admire the beachcombing life, even to yearn for it. The inventive spirit of the beachcomber lies deep in our race memory, scanning with some ancient animal instinct to hunt with the eye the line of tide wrack, searching for any useful or interesting item, anything with which to improvise, delight or create.

Significant objects I have found while beachcombing include the Yellow 8-Knots Buoy and the Sea Leopard. What is a sea leopard I hear you wonder? The *Sea Leopard* was the shark-fishing boat which belonged to Gavin Maxwell, bought unsighted and ill-advisedly for his doomed enterprise, Isle of Soay Shark Fisheries, the subject of his book, *Harpoon at a Venture*. The Sea Leopard is a noble animal of the imagination, with a noble association in the poet-adventurer collective memory, and yet it was moved by fate, with a choice of anywhere else in the world to go to, to come to me, here on our beach.

It was on one of my typical beachcombing excursions, which always accompany some other greater purpose of firewood-foraging, photography or greyhound exercising at the same time, that my eye was scanning the line of tide wrack when it alighted on some tiny yellow creature tangled and buried among the seaweed. Untangling this thing, it became clear that it was a small plastic leopard, obviously a homage to the original *Sea Leopard*, and coincidentally a dead ringer for Chuffy, the brindle greyhound now porpoising about the beach not far away, my own domestic sea leopard of a dog.

The Yellow 8-Knots Buoy was washed up one morning when the beach was absolutely clean smooth sand, all shingle having been removed by a recent tide, as happens here. The effect of the bright yellow on the empty beach was of a work of art; a famous photograph perhaps, or a painting with abstract tendencies. I dragged the Yellow 8-Knots Buoy off the beach and tied it to the post of the sign which warned of DANGER NO FOOTPATH, by the footpath at the edge of the cliff. It became a local landmark, a marker buoy showing the way onto the beach, and a sitting place.

When someone found a small piece of gravestone with part of its recognisable but illegible inscription intact, they placed it at the base of the post, so that the 8-Knots Buoy then became a sort of visual memorial to that unknown person in the minds of the locals, and as people sat on it and looked out to sea, perhaps they wondered about him, or her. Then one night the whole lot was unsentimentally washed away, so that was that.

The Yellow 8-Knots Buoy must still be somewhere out there in the world. It was quite big and very tough. I still feel guilty and half-responsible for that one item of ocean plastic, despite the number of two-minute beach cleans I must have done.

It is surprising how quickly and completely nature can transform a place visually; occasionally, as part of some natural disaster, more often in the course of a normal day: the 1953 flood; the 1987 storm; sunsets, lightning, rainbows, wind, fire, ice, snow. This sudden visual transformation happens quite regularly around our beach and cliff-top territory and it is difficult not to be held in thrall to the intriguing effects.

The white glare of fresh snow over the farmland, combined with a bright reflecting sea and a still-frozen beach, all reflected and exaggerated by the sun and the sky, is a particularly wondrous landscape to behold and all the more so for its rarity. Of all things bright and beautiful, snow on the beach in sunlight is almost blindingly bright.

Not long ago, I was collecting firewood from a series of tides which had brought in quite a haul of small broken planks, perhaps from a smashed pallet or crate of some sort. I had stacked these under the cliff and began to head back to the house with the first load, intending to return for the remainder as I find it more unpleasant to carry heavy loads than to make return trips (a terrible dilemma of survival which must have haunted our ancestors frequently). There was quite a breeze, but nothing out of the ordinary for an English beach in early spring, when suddenly there began a sort of whirlwind just ahead of me.

I had seen this kind of localised mini-tornado during a past adventure in Jordan, a desert adventure 'in the footsteps of Lawrence of Arabia' involving a group of forty nameless numbered Arab horses in Wadi Rum. Then, several mini-tornadoes had whipped up in separate places, all visible as clear columns of sand, cleanly sucked up into separate vortices from the surface, but moving around the desert like sandy whirling dervishes with that slightly wobbly wiggle you see on an imperfect potter's wheel, and all rather beautiful.

As is so often the case, this display of natural beauty also held within it a veiled threat. Only this time it was us, not the threat, who should have been veiled, as the whole of the immediate desert suddenly erupted into a full-blown sandstorm. We hunkered down with our faces and eyes wrapped up, huddled within the protection of our red-and-white kaffiyehs, and in that instant we understood completely why as shepherds we had worn tea-towels on our heads in nativity plays. The kaffiyeh is a practical item in sun and sandstorm and makes a good drying-up cloth too.

Then, as suddenly as it had started, the sandstorm stopped; but the whole landscape seemed a slightly different shape, disorientating and with a palpable warning unspoken in the air, along the lines of, *if you were all alone here in this desert, you would be lost very soon, and you would die.* Sudden remodelling of the landscape can occur in the sea of dunes of the Sahara, in which even the local Berbers and Bedouin can be fatally lost. But the romance of the Arabian sands became all the greater for our intimacy with those stinging grains and we briefly basked in the high-drama-afterglow of the seasoned adventurer.

Armed with this vivid and quite exciting memory, I surveyed the little whirlwind before me on the beach with interest. But before I could say 'Salaam alaikum; yalla, yalla!' (as I believe is normal in a desert in a sandstorm), I was transported into the three-dimensional wide-screen version of the complete sandstorm scene, cast romantically in the role of Lawrence of Arabia himself, trudging through the bright ochres of the desert, leaning into the salt-wind lashing against my face, now almost invisible amid all the sand in the air as it was blown up by the winds and whirlwinds. And again, after another few seconds of extreme visual transformation, it suddenly stopped; and I was back on a Suffolk beach, albeit a slightly different beach from the one I had left only minutes before. Scenes such as this are extraordinary to us and yet so ordinary to nature. These rearranging events must occur frequently and without witness, as unseen as the avalanches in the silent high Andes.

These sudden visual transformations are not confined to any particular medium, as is evident from another recent 'visual event' from within our territory.

I was driving home over the reedbed road near Mardle Lane (mardle being Suffolk for chat in a gossipy manner) when I came upon a gathering of vehicles, as if some frightful accident had befallen several people at the same time and at the same corner. Imagining silent drownings and fen-like sinking cars, my mind began its machinations, think clearly what to do, and how most effectively to save someone from such a fate. Then I was brought to a halt by a crowd of people with enormous long lenses, as if they had just spotted Prince Harry and his wife in the bulrushes. There were more of these long-lensed people arrayed all along the bank, so I followed the direction of their lenses.

Murmurations of starlings gathering to roost are quite a frequent sight here and the best sightings are not necessarily the biggest, but the ones seen unexpectedly, or alone. Nevertheless, these people clearly knew that they were on to something big and had evidently been alerted to it by human tweets. They were understandably transfixed by the sight and noise of these unimaginable numbers of birds, swooping and swirling about in their giant amorphous forms, filling the skies. I felt grateful to this bird-watching tribe, despite their blocking of the road, for not having had a terrible accident after all, but instead accidentally drawing my attention to this wondrous sight.

While watching the birds, the bird-watchers seemed at the same time distracted from actually looking, and they were not observing this wonder of the natural world with complete immersion in the moment. Taunted by the tyranny of their telescopes and technology, and by the need to record rather than simply to *see*, to a man (and they were all men) they viewed the whole event through the distancing barrier of a lens, a very long lens, which somehow seemed a pity.

Blocked by all their cars and generally avoiding crowds, I nipped up Mardle Lane to escape the human hordes, who were by now themselves massing in the manner of a murmuration.

In the wide skies over our cliff, the full visual effect of the murmuration became infinitely and engrossingly watchable. Enormous and ever-growing amoeba forms were lava-lamping and swirling, expanding here, then contracting and lengthening, then suddenly swooping in shoals and geometries of amorphous architecture in three dimensions all over the sky. No-one bumped into anyone and no-one seemed to hesitate in their chosen path. We are told that each bird has to look out for cues from the seven nearest others to know which way to go next. But while this may be true, it does no justice to the sheer poetry of the visual event and the experience. And after all that magnificence, a performance for no applause except their collective and individual survival, all the little birds went to bed.

The famous illness of Monsieur Henri Beyle is a disorder acknowledged by medical science and known to history as Stendhal Syndrome. It identifies the symptoms suffered by aesthetes who are overexposed to beauty, who actually overdose on beauty, the original case being that of a man who was overwhelmed and rendered helpless by an overdose of Renaissance art in Florence. We must raise a glass to this man, for the effects of such extra-appreciation must have afflicted our ancestors since the first beauty-sensitive caveman-aesthete emerged from his lair, yet only now is it all right to secretly admit to being made to cry by the architecture of a Venetian church, as I did when I first stood under the centre of the dome of the Salute, or by the sight of a group of little birds putting themselves to bed in a Suffolk sky. 'Stendhals Anonymous' would be the loveliest group of self-help afflictees ever to assemble. I must join.

The nature of visual camouflage is a fascinating subject, with 'disruptive pattern' being the operative words. The art of not being seen is all about breaking up the expected visual cues, so as not to isolate the individual in any given context, multiple-zebra-style, and it must be said that a brindle greyhound on a shingle beach does this most admirably. Nature is the absolute master of camouflage and disguise, but brindle is the artistic zenith. The fascinating aspect of brindle is that it can render a large and excitable dog like Chuffy invisible in so many different terrains. The army could learn from this.

Chuffy the Brindle Bomber is not the most disciplined of dogs at the best of times, so if he goes for a canter it can be somewhat disquieting, for the canter of an ex-racing greyhound (of 96 races'-worth of experience, not counting the training) covers the ground very efficiently. This does not mean *fast* as in a real sprint burst, just a loping wolf-pace which is difficult to keep up with by any method other than Land Rovering. Being brindle, he also becomes invisible in the process of his loping, whether on plough or stubble, shingle or sand. He can even disappear in woodland. This is a remarkable visual feat for a dog. And a very annoying one.

In the reedbeds, nature has given the bittern a similarly

versatile brindled cloak, all painted with Vs, but this rare and elusive bird also performs a rather remarkable conjuring trick to make certain of the efficacy of his disguise. If the bittern is alarmed, the visual part of its defence is to stick its beak straight up vertically in a stunningly clever impersonation of a reed. Stuffed and mounted under a glass dome in a Victorian taxidermy collection, this might not be too impressive as a disguise; but once placed *in situ* in the reedbeds, I imagine it must be very effective. I don't know exactly how perfect his disguise is in context, because I've never actually spotted the bittern in the reedbeds, only flying heron-like in that general direction. Which rather proves the point.

'I didn't see you at camouflage training this morning.'

'Thank you, Sir.'

(From *Dear Lupin* by Roger and Charlie Mortimer)

While sandstorms, murmurations and the magical qualities of brindle are visually fascinating in their own right, they are by definition part of nature's ongoing rhythms and rites. Occasionally, there occurs such a dramatic one-off visual drama that it stays in the collective memory for years, decades and even centuries, becoming a sort of folkloric local parable to be told and retold, warped and distorted by memory and exaggeration. The 1953 flood is one such event; the 1987 storm another. We have our own, more recent folkloric tale to tell, and it happened on the beach right under the Easternmost House.

One morning, the coastal people of East Anglia woke up to an extraordinary sight. The visual anomaly was spread along many miles, including all of the Suffolk coast and in particular the whole unbroken length of our beach. We have seen odd invasions before, of starfish, of jellyfish, and of a type of seaweed resembling lengths of ragged home-made linguine. But on this memorable occasion, we were greeted at dawn by what became known as the Timber Tide.

As we sea-people started to go about our habitual early-morning outdoor activities, dog-walking and animal feeding, we individually suddenly spotted it, each separately aghast, as if it was our own single discovery. Along the entire line of the last high tide, washed up overnight there was a ragged barricade of an unimaginable enormity of tangled lengths of sawn timber, all piled up and strewn about along the entire length of the beach and stretching far beyond the distant vanishing points to north and south. That ship that had been reported as breaking up in the English Channel, and which we had rather forgotten about, had very evidently and finally broken up after all. And now, here on our beach, appeared to be the entire cargo of that ill-fated vessel.

At first, we were all simply curious, like the bemused inhabitants of some Polynesian tribe of spear-fishermen who have just woken up to find the Royal Yacht Britannia unexpectedly moored to their jetty, and who are now being approached by the heavily-guarded and garlanded Queen and Duke of Edinburgh. Then there came a stage of amusement at the sheer visual spectacle arrayed before us. Finally, there came a kind of exhilaration, a wood-wonderment: we were lumber-drunk, plank-happy, beaming. It was amazing and very, very primitive. The blood of our ancestors coursed through our veins.

Here, the moral dilemmas which might have presented themselves, seemed cleanly and simply absent. No-one had deliberately led the ship onto rocks to harvest its loot. There were no finished man-made products, no valuable components of industry, no packaging or labels marking anything as belonging to Someone Identifiably Else, no food, no clothes, not even any drugs or alcohol. Nothing to induce guilt at all. Just wood. Masses and masses of wood.

Timber Galore.

MARCH

Food in season and local 'sea state' update

Veg
Purple sprouting broccoli, calabrese, spring greens, cabbage

Game
Pigeon, rabbit, hare, muntjac

Fish
Wild salmon, sea trout, seasons can vary in different areas/rivers, Scotland, Wales etc.
15th March - 6th Oct: wild brown trout

Distance from cliff
22 metres, with large chunks eating into the barley field to the south

Change since last month
No change, but jagged edge and small losses along cliff path to beach

Lanterns on the Beach

Keep my hands from picking and stealing...

The Book of Common Prayer

4

APRIL

'Oh, to be in England, now that April's there, for whoever wakes in England sees, some morning, unaware, that the lowest boughs of the brushwood sheaf the elm tree bowl are in tiny leaf, while the chaffinch sings in the orchard bough, in England – now!' One of the earliest poems I learnt as a punishment for talking after lights-out at boarding school, was *Home Thoughts from Abroad*, by Robert Browning. At that time, it was one of my favourite poems (another being the 'Stop all the clocks' one made famous in *Four Weddings and a Funeral*, which I also learnt as a 'punishment'). Now, reading the April poem aloud as fluent normal English without the line breaks (as above, and in the game of 'Crit that Poet'), it niggles me that Robert Browning has used the word 'bough/s' twice in the same sentence and has ended the poem with a gratuitously unnecessary screamer!

Yet the April poem and its sentiment still evokes in me

a nostalgia for certain 'old friends' who have died, old friends who happened to be trees: a particular weeping lime felled by the 1987 storm, our lost orchards, an old chestnut. The weeping lime I planted as a teenager, mourning the many losses in the storm, is now thriving and tall. I remember feeling guilty for minding more about the weeping lime than some person who had recently died at the time. I find it comforting to think how many long-lived trees I have personally planted during my brief moment of life, like the wise man of the aphorism, who plants trees in whose shade he will never sit.

Browning's poem also stirs a more general appreciation of our native trees, particularly the English elm, many an 'elm tree bowl' savaged by Dutch Elm Disease, approximately when we were toddlers. It reminds us of our symbiotic relationship with wood and timber, the 'if we nurture trees, they will nurture us' kind of idea, and how cut timber is so obviously useful. More of which later.

As well as brushwood sheaf in tiny leaf and the Grand National (by far the most exciting day of the year for me when aged ten), April on our clifftop also brings the 'stringing of the beach', which involves the stringing-off of a section of shingle for the ground-nesting birds. Avocets, oystercatchers and ringed plovers nest there undisturbed, by the calm water of Easton Broad, which is also visited by bitterns, geese, mallards and swans.

There is a movement in the birdwatching world, a world with which I am largely unfamiliar (despite watching birds most days) promoting birdwatching as beneficial to mental health. Although mental health is a currently fashionable subject, my hunch is that mental health problems have always been with us and always will be, and not everyone can stiff-upper-lip their way through it, so anything that helps people deal with their troubles can only be a good thing. And watching birds certainly can.

I hesitate to use the word 'birdwatching', as it leads into 'birding' and then 'twitching' and phrases like 'showing well', which can become mildly obsessive, even to the point of aggression. I know this because I have several times met unexpected birders in our so-called garden, looking into the hedge from the garden side not the crop side (which is also private land) for a tree sparrow or some other little brown job they have been alerted to by Rare Bird Alert on the internet. The birders were enthusiastic and chatty, but apart from trespassing, which people are perfectly free to do, it seems slightly bad manners to actually go into someone's garden without asking. The 'right to roam' applies to uncultivated mountain and moorland, not the gardens of Suffolk. Serious birding also seems to miss some of the point.

Concentrating on quantifying rather than qualifying birds, ticking-off rather than just enjoying watching the birds for their own sake, seems to create extra stress rather than calming it. It strays into avian trainspotting. Will the bird 'show well'? Can we flush the bird? Why are we not allowed on this private land? And all of this in a big crowd of people with long lenses. The now infamous 'PG Tips twitch' at Holkham is a fine example of the genre, immortalised on YouTube.

Birds often cited as rare or endangered, particularly hen harriers, lapwings and curlews, are living quite happily here, untagged, unwatched, unseen by anyone, except occasionally by me and three ducks. Reed buntings are regulars in our garden. Sand martins live in deep holes in the cliff. Swooping swallows and sand martins seem to lose some of their freedom when referred to as 'hirundines', and a swift is a swift is a swift. Birdwatching somehow seems more stressful than simply watching birds. While the chaffinch sings on the orchard bough, thoughts return to the affair of the timber tide.

When any cargo ship breaks up, it creates a mini adventure but also a problem. On our coast, a chaotic line of sawn timber lengths, all about 3 metres long, with differing cross-sections, giving the habitual anomaly of 3 metres of 4 by 2 (inches), or 4be2, was overnight stretched out in a tangled mass along the beach into the far distance beyond any vanishing point. We were immersed in a major wrecking drama of tremendous instinctive human interest, but already presenting practical difficulties. This amount of timber was so enormous that quite quickly it became clear that it would be a hell of a job to shift it off the beach. And it would also present a terrible hazard to small boats if we did not. At this point we rather wished that we could bring in the army.

We had enough timber to build ourselves cathedrals

and sea defences, barns and stables and chicken houses, and houses for ourselves with private piers and landing stages, and the boats that we would wish to moor to these structures, and whatever other creations we might imagine. Anything at all, as long as it was buildable in timber. But we lacked manpower. We rewound through several centuries of societal evolution and surprisingly early on in the process, our thoughts turned to our collective manpower and our collective assets: Land Rovers, tractors and trailers, horseboxes, and horses for that matter. Horses are still used in forestry.

The jungle telegraph of our primitive ancestors rumbled loudly and quite soon there was a straggle of curious observers. The fascination of our early morning discovery became the leading news story, locally and nationally; and after that came the invasion.

'Don't Take A Fence', said one of the first headlines and the jungle telegraph rumbled again, so that by osmosis we all instantly became experts about wreck and salvage law, notifying the Receiver of Wreck and so on. Enlightenment dawned that this is how it must have happened at times over history. A kind of crisis, whether beneficial or adverse, would prompt a burst of initiative-taking and knowledge-finding, which would last and be useful for the next time. But each burst would be followed by a long plateau of nothing in particular needing to be invented or learned.

The cargo was apparently from the Russian-registered *Sinegorsk*, and once the news was broadcast, the crowds came, to salvage, to watch, or just to be on telly in the evening. First, local tractors and trailers, followed by horseboxes, Mighty Jimnys and Land Rovers, then pick-up trucks and finally, the serious white vans from distant towns and cities. Any and all modern equivalents of the strongest farm horse and 'waggon' turned up to collect their haul. This was a clear case of salvage, washed-up bounty, beachcombing writ large, and no-one had any compunction about making the most of this gift from nature, a pattern which must have been known to coastal peoples all over the world, since the dawn of time.

As people were turning up in all sorts of trucks and cars to collect their timber, others came simply to see the spectacle. This was quite an interesting story in itself, but the really fascinating part of it, is what followed.

Gradually and without any bossiness or official leadership of any kind, clusters and teams of people started forming to help each other. This co-operation was partly for fun and partly because of a shared sense of necessity and urgency, to save the timber and to clear up the potentially dangerous mess on the beach, which would be lethal to the small fishing boats in our harbour if the tide flung it back into the sea. And what a waste of a timber opportunity that would be.

Once again, as we co-operated, we rewound through centuries of evolution and discovered for ourselves the value of the human chain, and the extremely useful innovation of putting knots in a length of rope when pulling a weight upwards hand-over-hand. And at this point we decided to invent gloves, at least we would have done so, if our ancestors hadn't sensibly and kindly already done it for us.

By mid-afternoon we resembled a well-drilled army exercise designed to illustrate the benefits of teamwork to untrained new recruits. Yet there was no boss and no-one barking orders with a megaphone, nor was there any safety officer, nor any high-viz clothing, nor any hard hats. There were no rules, no votes, no arguments. We were just a practical muddle of be-gloved and be-roped human chains, ranging across the beach.

Underneath the Easternmost House, our human chain was aided by a cliff-top team of receiving hands and we passed many happy hours, just passing pieces of timber to each other, hand to hand, touch to touch, again and again. No-one fought over it, no-one squabbled, no-one went on strike, no-one complained. No-one even stopped for tea. It was a truly fascinating education. One wondered where and when and how in our history, things had gone so wrong since this harmonious stage in our evolution. Later, as the dusk began to fall, torches began miraculously to appear.

Once it became established as evening, the scene along the shoreline was transformed. The light of the torches was gradually augmented by the lighting of fires and lanterns along the beach. We then became a piece of living history, wreckers from the days of yore, passing the timber, person to person, hand to hand, and up the cliff, to be grabbed by the receiving hands at the top.

We were like the dark shadows in an old painting of

wreckers from three centuries ago, silhouetted figures working together, illuminated by the flickering lights of fires and lanterns on the beach. This was a scene for which the word *chiaroscuro* could have been invented. We seemed timeless yet historical, not really from the world of today at all.

In that firelight, with the wind and tide turning, and the waves crashing on the shingle in the darkness, and the background roar of the sea all around us, we could have been from any century, or from prehistory itself. In a modern world that encourages sedentary virtual experiences, and values social networks made up of unknown friends, here was as real a physical experience and palpable a social interaction as was possible to imagine. The blood of our ancestors coursed through our veins again. We were animals.

We passed the timber, person to person, hand to hand, almost as a meditation.

APRIL

Food in season and local 'sea state' update

Veg
Spring cabbage, carrots, end of root veg and sprouts

Fruit
Height of rhubarb season, strictly a vegetable

Game
Pigeon, rabbit, hare, muntjac

Meat
Lamb

Fish
Crabs, lobster, shrimp, salmon, trout

Eggs
1st April - 15th May, gulls' eggs, strictly regulated and
by licence only

Distance from cliff
22 metres

Change since last month
No change, but jagged edge and small losses along
cliff path to beach

1st April - 31st August
Hedge-cutting off-season, not allowed again
until September

Fur, Feather, Fin, Fire and Food

The generations of living things pass in a short time, and, like runners, hand on the torch of life. What is food to one man is bitter poison to others.

De Rerum Natura
Lucretius (99-55 BC)

5

MAY

It is interesting to see how differently wild animals respond to humans when we are on a horse. We become more primitively animal on a horse. I have ridden on the beach and around the landscape of this part of Suffolk, on and off, all my life, from the cherished joys of Pony Club Camp in Henham Park, now famous for pink sheep and the Latitude Festival, to pragmatically being paid to exercise other people's horses to get them fit. In Wadi Rum, on horses, the wild camels and wild oryx were unafraid of us. In Suffolk, I have occasionally seen the magical, mythical sight of a white hart, and always the horse was the catalyst, my cover, my camouflage and my ally. Our ancestors must have seen the white hart's ancestors too and celebrated by naming the pub in Blythburgh after it.

The Suffolk safari around our clifftop is not confined to land, river and sea. The sky is a rewarding hunting ground for watching the wild. There was much local dissent a few years ago when there was a proposal to release sea eagles along this coast. There were fears that the sea eagles would take piglets and lambs. There may be a sinister long-forgotten reason why so many pubs are called The Eagle and Child. A sparrowhawk once swooped down on our garden and killed a pigeon and there are alleged to be wild goshawks about the place, although I'm not sure I would recognise one without Helen MacDonald's menacing *H is for Hawk* book cover picture as a field guide.

The Hen Reedbeds are a haven for secretive creatures. The hovering marsh harrier casts a shadow over the unsuspecting frogs and mice in the long grass at the edge of the crops and I remain convinced that I once saw a bird of prey flying alongside the track dangling a cat from his talons. People always say it must have been a rabbit, but if it had been a rabbit, surely, I would have just thought, oh dear, poor bunny, rather than being startled and fascinated by the fact of it being a cat? Cats, oddly the pet of choice among some vegan animal rights activists, allegedly kill about 275 million wild animals and birds a year in the UK, according to a report by the Mammal Society. Clearly it is not the cats' fault, hunting and play-killing being in their nature, but to inflict so many non-native predators on our own native wildlife seems an unnecessary carnage, a paradox full of pathos. Whichever bird of prey swooped down on that ill-fated cat would have saved many more lives than it took that day.

The local territory of the Easternmost House is possibly the only place on earth where you can be served smoked eel in a public place, for pudding, without a murmur. Some time ago, when we went out to dinner, as opposed to just eating it outside, we chose as a first course 'smoked local eel with beetroot and horseradish', which turned out to be an artistic creation including crème fraiche and shards of colour alongside the eel. One of us liked this combination so much that after the long-forgotten middle course, he asked for some more 'smoked local eel with beetroot and horseradish', for pudding. Yes, sir. Of course, sir. People eat smoked eel for pudding here all the time, sir. Quite normal. Quality service from The Swan in Southwold, and not a giggle.

The story of these local eels, who were treated with such double-reverence at the table, is one of nature's marvels, a great ritual of migration and survival. The elvers, which are the size of bootlaces, apparently make the journey from the Sargasso Sea in the north Atlantic to the rivers of East Anglia, including our river. They then stay in these rivers for fifteen years until they are mature, by which time they are about three or four feet long. Then suddenly, out of the blue, by some magic of nature, they wake up one morning knowing, *knowing* by instinct, that they must now set off on the journey back to the Sargasso Sea to lay eggs. How, *how*, can that be? Inevitably, human life threatens this extraordinary wonderment of migration. Changes in habitat, water quality, climate change, global warming, diversion of the gulf stream and so on, threaten the eels in their already mighty quest.

On your imaginary pocket-cottage visits to the

Easternmost House, you will find yourself surrounded by good food of all sorts, much of it produced within a five-mile radius, for this is a region especially celebrated for the quality and variety of its food and drink. We still have plenty of roadside honesty boxes selling eggs, asparagus, honey or jam, because people are honest and pay. We still have independent butchers' shops, because people will still buy the old-fashioned, slow-cooking, nose-to-tail, cheap cuts of meat, as well as the more obvious offerings favoured by supermarkets. We still have fishermen and a working harbour because we buy fish from our fishermen's huts. Local and seasonal is the thing, rather than organic or over-hyped or over-priced. Ordinary fresh fruit and veg, not billed as 'plant-based' when they are just plants. Things chopped up, not spiralised. Normal fresh greenery, not clean eating. Timeless, obvious, unfashionable food.

Our immediate territory is also as fine a place as any to essay and foray in search of wild food, in fur, feather, fin and field. There is an abundance of animals surrounding us within a one-mile radius of our clifftop, some seen, some secretive. One of the tragedies of the world today is the separation of so many people from physical contact with other animals, seeing them only in a picture on a screen. Whether in the wild, or in our fields, or in our houses, animals are our allies. Animals are an example to us, with their ability to live in the present moment and their blessed lack of anxiety about the past or the future. Animals have a calm amorality about them, which means they cannot actively and intentionally be evil or cruel. Animals do whatever they do because they need to, or just because they do. Animals decorate the landscape with their presence. They animate the silence with their odd sounds. They amuse us with their odd habits. Animals have the capacity to show emotions of joyfulness and misery, and they can certainly feel pain. We have a duty to treat animals well, but as at least 97% of us are also happy to eat them, or food derived from them, animals also lead into temptation, and into some awkward corners of moral philosophy.

Animals have individual characters, or if they don't, they seem to. It is slightly disturbing to observe the behaviour of domestic chickens closely. Knowing your own chickens can lead to a stale dark place: seeing clearly the potential for cruelty inherent in intensive poultry farming. Among the various chickens we have kept as companionable domestic egg-layers over the years, all of them have displayed what one could call a personality, an individual character: Pud was a motherly fat hen, Sab always seemed rather angry, Shy Baby was perpetually anxious, Moderate and Good were ordinary-looking Skyline hens who laid beautiful blue eggs and Cockle, the cock, was like a perfectly-mannered avuncular old gent pottering about at the Garrick Club.

Clucky and Debo (named after the late, great chicken-loving Dowager Duchess of Devonshire) were a little bantam husband and wife team, who jumped into my arms in the morning and sat on the table while we ate. Clucky and Debo taught us the secret of a happy marriage: just wanting to be together. When distracted by their scratching perambulations, one or other would suddenly notice that their beloved was too far away and run over, just to be nearer, to be together. Clucky and Debo were pets, tragically killed by the farm black Labrador, whose breeding and instincts had been honed over centuries to retrieve feathered game, but who lacked the reputed 'soft mouth' that is supposed to be characteristic of good gundogs. If eight domestic chickens can display these diverse qualities, each a distinct and memorable chicken-character, almost a little chicken-soul, so, logically, can the farmed and factory-farmed chickens who are their closest relations. It is disquieting.

Pud, Sab, Shy Baby, Moderate, Good, Cockle, Clucky and Debo all seemed to experience the following sensations quite markedly: warmth and cold, and comfort or discomfort resulting from either, something like cheerfulness, or at least being pleased to see the hand that brings the food, general background fear, and real immediate terror, relief when terror ends, independent decision-making of sorts, contentment and something similar to boredom. I know that these individual chickens would be denied a part of their natural behaviour if they were never to see the daylight or sun, living for only a few weeks in a large predator-proof shed. They would surely suffer if they were not stunned properly in the robotic killing-plucking-and-oven-readying factory process.

In addition to the most basic reflex sensations, chickens show every inclination towards enjoying human and other company. Pud the black rock hen was, for six years, improbably great friends with Speedy the Big Black Greyhound. Together, these two would sleep for hours at a time in Speedy's bed. When outside together, both hen and greyhound seemed to display something very like humour, although that might be going too far down the anthropomorphic route for the scientists and zoologists among you, but I once had a horse called Dotty who definitely had a sense of humour, and Chuffy seems to find it funny to run away, loping off just out of the comfortable radius, just for fun. A kind of humour seems to be among the observable range of animal emotions.

There is a commercial chicken shed nearby in which the ventilation broke down overnight. The following day, 20,000 chicken-bodies, each arguably a little chicken-soul like Pud, were scraped out and disposed of by bull-dozer, since these chickens were now 'not fit for human consumption'. But perhaps they never were 'fit for human consumption', morally. On the other hand, the chickens were never in danger of being eaten by a fox and factory farming since the war has provided cheap protein to a population who have never been so well nourished before. Some people are against other people shooting pheasants, which on our cliff, around our so-called garden and in the woods at Benacre live a relatively natural life, as well as being highly valued as food available from the butchers in all our local market towns. Yet we collectively (if not individually) are also happy to tuck into a chicken korma or a family bucket of finger-lickin' chicken from who knows where, one of 945 million chickens eaten every year in the UK. Food is our modern moral minefield, a labyrinth, a rabbit hole from which you can never escape, even if you go vegan.

At the far end of the clifftop where there is an area marked on OS maps as 'The Warren', there live many extended families of rabbits, with their cousins and second-cousins flopsy-bunnying about among the black cliff-sheep heading off towards the marshes, confounding reports of a rabbit crisis. Rabbit numbers are apparently down elsewhere, which is worrying. The cliff-sheep on have their own little beach hut surrounded by gorse and they sometimes escape their large enclosure to roam the cliffs. One-Horn, a ram, was tragically mauled by a summer-visiting lurcher, one of hundreds of cases of fatal 'sheep worrying' by loose dogs which go largely unreported in the press, and a euphemistic misnomer if ever there was one. It was in this general vicinity that I once watched a remarkable spring rabbit-and-lamb scene unfold before me.

A very young lamb was gambolling about in the spring sunshine (as only lambs ever seem to do) when a small baby rabbit hopped into the orbit of its activity. The baby rabbit was just snuffling about, twitching its nose, when the lamb skipped up to have a sniff of its twitchy nose. The baby rabbit hopped away and suddenly started racing round the lamb, who stood in the middle of the circle and jumped straight up in the air from a standing start on all fours, as lambs will at such moments. The baby rabbit raced round and round and then the lamb joined in. The lamb and the baby rabbit continued racing round and round and round, chasing each other for a sustained period of several minutes. They seemed to be doing this for the sheer fun of each other's company, and joy in the act of running, the whole scene like an extreme 'aaaah' moment set up by a school of sentimental film-making. Yet these adorable fluffy free-running happy creatures are also food. People shoot pigeons and rabbits as an agricultural pest and they also eat them. The thinking meat-eater and moral philosopher should logically prefer to eat the wild pigeon, or the lamb or the rabbit that has skipped in the sunshine, than the chickens from the stale dark shed, yet it is not so. We are a contrary and hypocritical species.

Rabbits don't like swimming, but hares have an extra layer of fur, so can occasionally be seen swimming across ditches and dykes. Possibly no other animal is so steeped in rural folklore as the brown hare. Hares are connected with the Goddess Eostre, and have all sorts of associations with the moon, fertility symbolism and the Easter Bunny. In East Anglian dialect, hares are known as sallies or stubble stags. The three-hare roundel is often found in church architecture. The brown hare is considered as native as the mountain hare now but was originally introduced by the Romans as a source of food and sport. Hares are unavoidably bound up with the history of the chase, with packs of harriers traditionally more common than foxhounds in East Anglia, their breeding still thriving albeit adapted to the hunting of an artificial trail, in line with modern sensibilities and law.

The noble history of the greyhound is also closely linked with that of the hare, coursing being an ancient sport. The greyhound appears in the Bible (Proverbs 30:31), Chaucer (the Monk and his greyhounds), Shakespeare (Henry V, Act 3, Scene 1, just before 'Cry "God" for Harry, England and Saint George!') and in our heraldry, art and architecture. Very often in these artistic depictions of greyhounds, there is a hare or a deer not far away, for the greyhound to pursue. Huntingfield church in Suffolk has painted greyhounds as hatchments on the wall, carved greyhounds on pews and stone greyhound gargoyles on a mausoleum attached to the church, all relating to the Vanneck family, formerly of nearby Heveningham Hall, whose emblem is a greyhound. Coincidentally, and dating from well before the greyhounds, there are stone harrier hound heads carved into the church window surrounds outside. The hare and the hunting of it, is deeply embedded in this part of Suffolk, even in the very name of the village: Huntingfield. The village sign shows a hare. This hunting field was never about the pursuit of the fox.

The agricultural monocultures of the 1970s are blamed for drastically reduced hare numbers, although large estates in East Anglia still hold annual hare shoots where the hares are sold into the human food chain as wild game. It is certainly true that in the golden summers of our childhood, we rode around the countryside on ponies amid scenes of unfathomable destruction, hedges uprooted and ponds filled in, the landscape ablaze with dangerous stubble-burnings. But the cultural tide has turned and hare populations are healthy in Suffolk.

I have often seen what at first appeared to be a huge

hare, which turned out to be a muntjac skipping lightly across the growing crops, covering the ground with astonishing grace and then vanishing into thin air, as wild animals do. Country people are inclined to remark on all sorts of undesirable features and habits of this peculiar little species of deer, all allegedly descended from some escapees from Woburn Abbey. People say muntjacs damage trees, eat bluebells, gore dogs with their tusks, damage crops and many other sins. But I once saw one of these beautiful animals, so perfect and skittish and lithe, suddenly jump out of the dark to be hit by a car some distance ahead, then run away into the night, probably injured. It seemed a tragedy of the highest order. There is, or should be, a sting to the human soul at the sight of a perfect animal damaged or killed. This is especially so if the animal is under our care, or if it is damaged by an accident of modern life from which even its sharpest natural instincts cannot possibly protect it.

There was an episode of *Countryfile*, the gentle Sunday-evening telly slot with an audience of about 8 million people, which featured a short piece about the overpopulation of deer in the UK and the need to cull them, followed by a lesson in butchering the resultant venison. It showed a normal piece of meat being cut up. Not the whole beast, no fur, no blood, no guts. There is a movement to introduce lynxes to cull the deer population near here, in a planned programme of rewilding. Similar ideas have been mooted for the Scottish Highlands, but with the addition of wolves. The lynxes are supposed to know that they must only eat the deer, not the ponies, foals, calves, piglets, lambs etc. Deer are shot as pests by professional stalkers, to avoid unbalanced overpopulation, so it seems odd to want to feed good quality venison to wolves and lynxes, with a chase to the death, when humans could eat it cleanly shot, but there you are. About 1% of the UK population is truly vegan, yet a small but significant minority of the meat-eating *Countryfile* audience took to Twitter on the night of the venison lesson, to be unusually offended and appalled at the butchering of meat that had lived a free and natural life as a deer. The offended section of the *Countryfile* audience would have been even more appalled if they had witnessed my own muntjac venison experience.

The moral dilemma arose when I came across a large and perfect adult muntjac lying freshly-killed on a remote road on the way to an architecture meeting. With hindsight, I probably should have stopped and moved the beast off the road for safety (of my fellow road-users not the muntjac), but I just drove round it to avoid being late for the elusive listed buildings officer. On the return trip, barely an hour later, the large muntjac was still there, still perfectly clean and fresh, so I did what any of our ancestors would have done. I thought of the quantity and quality of the protein before me. I thought of how meat was rationed in World War 2, and how Granny told me that Mr Keefy, the beloved Irish wolfhound and a kind of noble great uncle figure to me, had to be put down because he ate too much meat and it was deemed immoral to keep him. I thought of all the people in the world for whom this would be an undreamed of and necessary feast. It seemed borderline immoral to leave the muntjac there for the foxes or magpies or crows, just moving it out of the way of the road. So I put it in the boot of the Mighty Jimny, my rustic jeep-like car, and took it home to do it justice, with a certain reverence, and considerable regret for the untimely loss of its life at the hands of modern traffic.

With some trepidation but a clear idea of what to do, I took it to a quiet corner quite far from the house and hung it by its hind legs from a tree. With a working knowledge of the Stubbs's *Anatomy of The Horse* but having only ever skinned a few pheasants as a comparable test of practical butchery skills, I made the necessary cuts, creating a scene akin to Landseer keenly observing an NHS operating theatre as a live anatomy lesson. A few minutes later I had a large, neat pile of perfect venison meat. The remains, which included good quality offal protein that many humans would eat in certain circumstances, were left under the hedge for the foxes. I froze the neat and tidy venison meat and fed it to Chuffy, and us, for what seemed like weeks, a greyhound eating venison like the noble dog of some medieval king. But I had crossed a line. Come the apocalypse, or the desert island, or the plane crash, I might survive.

The wild larder around us includes all sorts of game birds and waterfowl, including a fat semi-tame pet woodpigeon called Poggi, pronounced Podgy, after a place we drove through in Tuscany and a semi-tame garden-pheasant called Fezzy. One sunny day, three downy young brindle-speckled birds came running down our track at full speed, chattering and chirping among themselves, and then screaming 'peep peep peep' as they headed straight towards the cliff at the end. At first glance, I assumed they were young partridges and I watched in horror as they paused briefly on the edge, before flinging themselves quite deliberately over the brink.

I have a peculiar fondness of partridges since once having some half-tame ones as sort-of pets, in the manner of Poggi The Podgy Pigeon and Fezzy, but tamer. The partridges laid eggs in the chicken house and followed me everywhere as if were a parent partridge, an endearing case of misplaced imprinting. So, feeling partridge-minded, I thought I'd try to see what on earth had become of these three little whatever-they-weres. I trotted along the cliff path and down on to the beach, hoping to help them, planning perhaps to pluck them from the cliff-side and return them to the top. In theory I disapprove of interfering with nature, but this time I had the idea that these three crazy little babies should be back where their parents would expect to find them. They seemed so young and fragile.

Of course, nature always knows best and the parents of these daring little teenagers must have given them some sign: It's time. Go. For when I found them, two of these tiny creatures had already scrabbled all the way down the crumbling cliff-face and were now bobbing happily about in a fairly rough sea, while the third had just completed his ragged descent and was racing across the beach to join them. These three little chums were evidently completely at home in this quite dangerous environment, which must have been all new and strange to them. They were not delinquent partridges at all. They must have been goslings of some sort. They were in their element. It was astonishing and oddly moving to see such tiny creatures, born to be wild geese and so inherently adapted and capable of just being wild geese. I understand that wildfowlers can also be naturalists and conservationists like Sir Peter Scott, who shoot and eat the birds they love and protect, but personally I couldn't do it. I am a partridge-and-goose-hypocrite.

On the farmland further away from the cliff-edge live a large number of free-range pigs, beach pigs, happy pigs, all outside in fresh air, snouting around in a favourite patch of mud. A few miles away at Blythburgh, there are even more free-range pigs, rumoured to be 24,000 pigs of all ages, award-winning free-range pork, bacon and sausages. Adorable galloping gangs of tiny piglets sometimes charge about for no apparent reason other than porcine *joie de vivre*, the many pig-families all living happily outside together with little Nissen-hut arks for houses. The big pigs chew on stones as part of their digestion process. Pigs seem to be very sociable, co-operative and contented creatures, an example to us all. They are a constant delight to see in the landscape.

Down on the marshes by the river, an assortment of old-fashioned and multi-coloured brown and dun cattle breeds provide ornament to the landscape and a background of contented mooing sounds. On other marshes, the red poll cattle graze, a breed that is one of the Suffolk Trinity, along with the Suffolk sheep and the Suffolk horse, whose colour is always chestnut, traditionally spelt 'chesnut', without the 't'. The future of this marshland livestock farming is uncertain, as the sea will come in over the land and the official line is that some places must be sacrificed to save others. 'Managed retreat' is the phrase. Hard places, meaning towns, will be saved and protected, but soft places, like our cliff or the marshland grazing, will not.

An escaped London entrepreneur has gradually bought several of the best local country houses and 4,500 acres of arable land near here. He has also planted millions of trees and employed plenty of local people. The whole enterprise has created a huge conservation project known as Wilderness Reserve, a remarkably ambitious enterprise on an epic eighteenth-century scale, which appropriately includes the restoration of a Capability Brown landscape, complete with new bridge (and twenty-first century tunnel under the road for the sheep). The grand plan is to gradually recreate habitats and accommodate future displaced wildlife when the sea comes in over the reedbeds and land. The whole project confounds those who complain about 'incomers'. All money was once new money. Incomers who spend their fortunes on doing this much local good are a godsend.

A pair of swans lives down on the marsh with the cattle, along the road leading from the water tower to the harbour and we have watched their family of cygnets grow up as if they were our own children. Swans are devoted and competent parents. They build a little island in a dyke, which at first looks rather exposed, but at exactly the right time, it vanishes into a wilderness of reeds, a swan-castle with a moat. Someone puts out a homemade sign of the rural variety every summer, when the cygnets are young and the tourists are here, with SLOW SWANS painted in messily swan-loving letters. The swans we cannot eat, even if we wanted to, which we don't, because they belong to the Queen, and only the Queen is allowed to eat her swans, and even then, only when they have been swan-upped at the annual swan-upping. Swans have cleverly managed to make it far too complicated to even contemplate categorising them as legally edible wild game.

Meat is the perpetual paradox, closely related to the paradox of the hunter and hunted and the degree to which individual people should be free to draw their own personal lines. If you want to know about an animal's behaviour, ask those who stalk it, shoot it, fish for it or farm it.

An old book, *The Encylopaedia of Sport*, is full of the most detailed natural histories of all the quarry species: roe deer, red deer, hare, rabbit, pheasant, partridge, wigeon, etc. Not long ago, until perhaps one or two generations ago, it would have been considered completely normal for *The Encyclopaedia of Sport* to contain A is for Archery, B is for Boxing, C is for Cricket, alongside A is for Air Rifle, B is for Beagling, C is for Coursing. Now, as the poem *The Fox's Prophecy* puts it, 'The vices of the town displace the pleasures of the field'. Some of these sports seem squalid to us now: C is for Cock Fighting, O is for Otterhound, but it will be a sad day when a man cannot teach his son to catch a fish without being called a murderer (of the fish) as some people earnestly believe he ought to be. 'Give a man a fish finger, and that is perfectly fine. Teach a man to fish, and he becomes an evil fish-murderer,' as the modern idiom might go.

This being Suffolk, and near Norfolk, we are surrounded by big farms and estates which support pheasant and partridge shooting. The best of them maintain woodland and high hedges and leave wide headlands round crops, and plant crops as cover for game. The habitats that benefit the pheasants and partridges evidently also benefit all sorts of other animals and birds. The dawn chorus on our clifftop, although entirely surrounded by arable land, reedbed, beach or sea, is reassuringly raucous. There is no silent spring here. There must be plenty of suitable habitat in the reedbeds and hedges, or we would not see so many reed buntings and different songbirds visiting our garden bird-feeders. The sound of skylarks fills the air all summer long.

Occasionally, a whole murmuration of starlings will descend on our garden in the early morning for some kind of invisible breakfast they must find there: birds all over the grass, birds along every branch of all the trees, birds along the telephone wires and birds along the outbuildings' roof ridges, birds everywhere, a scene really very like Hitchcock's *The Birds,* and only slightly less sinister. Then suddenly, with no apparent signal, a thousand starlings take off simultaneously and disappear into the clouds and we are left starling-startled, marvelling at nature's random wild madnesses.

In an increasingly overpopulated world, the moral maelstrom about how we feed ourselves is always just over the horizon. Vegans must hold some of the higher ground, commendable for their consistency and care, even if there are places in the world where people have to live entirely on reindeer, so to have the choice is itself a luxury. One of life's little mysteries is why the vegan foodstuff *Quorn* chose to name itself after one of the grandest foxhunts in the kingdom. Another of life's little mysteries is what to do with the male calves, kids, chicks etc. if we half-heartedly go vegetarian and eat milk, cheese and eggs but not meat.

At a party, an elegant cousin of the host wistfully lamented that she 'couldn't eat' any of the artistic little morsels, being vegetarian. At last, there came passing by, a little something with a sliver of goat's cheese about the size of a thumbnail, which she 'could eat'. But consider the billy-kids, thousands of them, killed at birth as a by-product of the goat's cheese industry, I thought. How can it be more moral to eat the tiny thumb-nail-sized morsel of goat's cheese, than to eat the unwanted billy-kids? In the future, I earnestly want to be a billy-kid farmer, building elaborate sham ruined castles and Palladian follies for the billy-kids to leap amusingly about on, before they become a niche, ethical, free-range cut of delicious and healthy meat, like a cross between venison and mutton. Cabrito Goat Meat, who already farm billy-kids as a by-product of the dairy industry, seem to be my only rivals. *What casual waste of life for a thumb-nail of goat's cheese. Ideally there would be hundreds of billy-kid farmers, and if we eat the goat's cheese, perhaps we should be prepared also to eat the billy-kids who spring directly from the process of making it.* Such were my thoughts as I smiled politely, and talked and laughed and listened and chatted to the elegant goat-muddled cousin of the host at the party. Or perhaps I was the one who was goat-muddled.

There was understandable uproar among vegans when Jammy Dodgers changed the recipe to include milk protein, yet Jammy Dodgers contain palm oil, a crop which according to the Worldwide Fund for Nature (or World Wildlife Fund, or WWF) causes the destruction of virgin rainforest at a rate equivalent of clearing the area of 300 football pitches *an hour*, which must do far more damage to many more species through loss of habitat than the milking of dairy cows. The dilemma of the Jammy Dodger puts the paradox of piglets and pigeon-shooting in perspective.

If all of Suffolk were suddenly to become vegan, the free-range pigs and marsh cattle would disappear from the landscape, then livestock farmers and stockmen and finally the knowledge. The Suffolk Show would be bereft and lifeless. Instead of eating sustainable protein from down the road, we might have to import soya and pulses to replace it, to achieve the bulk, possibly deforesting the Amazon rainforest and burning aviation fuel in the process. Farm animals belong in the English landscape. They have formed it. The fields and hedges and stone walls are there because of centuries of animal husbandry.

Although I am an eat-less-eat-better meat-eater, it is clear that if we want to preserve little piglets and rare breeds of farm animals, we must eat them. Jacob sheep used to be a rare breed but were paradoxically saved by being eaten. We could revisit the old-fashioned habits of even our recent ancestors: using the whole beast, nose to tail, wasting nothing, producing meat more kindly, less intensively, eating less of it. We could shake off our food taboos and eat an abundance of grey squirrels and muntjac and rook pie. We could be less squeamish.

People are intelligent enough to come to their own conclusions about how to feed themselves, and where to draw their own personal lines in the shifting sands and moral mole hills, but the Suffolk landscape surrounding the Easternmost House is more than scenery or a view, it is a significant proportion of the nation's home-grown food, and the disparate people who live and work on the land here on an agricultural scale (including me, working with horses, sheep, apples, vineyards and agricultural buildings), tend to have an abiding respect for legacy and tradition and for their animals.

We need to meet our meat and be able to look the animals squarely in the eye. We need to exercise restraint and add a reverent metaphorical handful of rosemary for remembrance. The crackling camp-fires of our ancestors, which long ago transformed the human relationship with other animals forever, still spit and burn in our instincts.

Is there anything, anything in the world, more uplifting than a high English hedge in May, bursting with blackthorn blossom, with clouds of cow parsley frothing at its base and perhaps a wild orchid here and there if you look carefully? Cancel the mowers until the end of August. Rural roadside verges are a million miniature nature reserves.

On the coast, cow parsley gives way to alexanders, called 'angelica' locally, which looks similar to cow parsley but is greener and less pretty. Angelica is the source of the sugary little green sticks which used to be commonly available for decorating cakes, but unsurprisingly are now virtually unknown. It is also alleged to be edible as vegetable, at least according to those foraging books. My only thought is that if it was really any good, we'd be farming it already, or on-trend London chefs would be begging us to pick it as a crop. The comparison of cow parsley with angelica makes the cow parsley seem even more beautiful, as it can't be taken for granted on the coast.

At Covehithe, a walkable distance to the north of our cliff but only accessible by road because of private land and cliff-falls relating to the Benacre estate (plus I don't want to encourage trespassers), the parish church is contained within the romantic ruin of a larger church, silhouetted against the sky, and surrounded by free-range pigs. The same church-within-its-larger-ruin history (plus nearby free-range pigs) is true of Walberswick. We are a declining population, less God-fearing than our wool-rich forbears. If you walk through the Covehithe graveyard and through the romantic ruin in May, there is a secret place where the cow parsley grows as if at its own festival in celebration of being cow parsley. Untouched by either human activity or grazing animals, this is a cow parsley paradise. A photography safari can never do it justice, but for the cow parsley curious, I have posted a photograph which should be findable on the magic internet, imaginatively titled 'Cow parsley at Covehithe'.

Our landscape turns yellow in May, as oilseed rape ripens. Rapeseed oil is quite fashionable, now that we are all apparently going vegan and caring about food miles (apart from all the imported almond milk and soya, obviously), but inexplicably it is more expensive than olive oil. People with hayfever start suffering now and they won't stop suffering until late September. Just when the hayfever sufferers think it's all over with the flowers and pollen, great clouds of harvest dust block out the sun as efficiently as the roaring combines drown out the birdsong.

Hayfever provoked by our crops seems to be a genuine problem for many of our visitors, while we who live and work here seem to be immune. Farmers sometimes grow agricultural-scale borage and linseed, as well as the ubiquitous oilseed rape, the latter of which covers hundreds of acres of this part of Suffolk. Flowers are completely unavoidable, so we seem to have evolved a built-in immunity if we grow up here. Just as in the 'olden days', farmers' wives deliberately left their babies' forearms unwashed, to boost their immunity, as a child I would clean out the guinea pigs, groom a pony, clean the tack and then pick and eat an apple, without washing my hands at any stage in the process, unless interrupted by lunch or church (which seemed to be a constant interruptive inconvenience to all my projects in those days). Admittedly this state of being unwashed was not consciously to boost my immune system, but the anecdotal evidence of my 0 days 'off sick' would suggest that it works. Unless it is a combination of genetic luck and self-employment, whereby the need to keep earning might be the spur to uncanny levels of good health.

As well as carpets of woodland bluebells nearby, we also have large areas of deliberately planted wildflowers and birdseed sunflowers on the farm. The edge of the cliff where it is not safe to plough also allows the embedded seeds to grow, resulting in a wildflower mix that could illustrate the bumper edition of the *Observer's Book of Wildflowers*. The planted wildflowers and sunflowers are classed as 'habitat land', along with the areas left as grass and native wildflowers, which are breeding grounds of lapwings and curlews. A grassy area further down the cliff near the reedbeds must also be home to mice and voles, as there are always barns owls and other birds of prey quartering it at certain times of day, including hen harriers. While this is all very beneficial to wildlife, it is a hayfever sufferer's nightmare.

To make it worse, I gather the seeds, mixing them into what Dame Miriam Rothschild called Farmers' Nightmare (an idea initiated by HRH The Prince of Wales in the early days at Highgrove), and spread the pretty weeds, or wildflowers, still further, because they add beauty and they help the bees. Self-seeding foxgloves and feverfew seem worthy of the herbaceous borders of a grand country house yet are considered weeds by some. Poppies begin to appear on the clifftop, and as I have left much of the so-called lawn to grow, a patchwork of tiny flowers has appeared.

You know your farming is 'extensive' when there's birdsfoot trefoil growing in the middle of the farm tracks. And there is. At night the poppies and tiny flowers fold their petals in the fading light, a process I have discovered is called nycinasty. 'Nycinasty' is one of those words, like 'triglyph' or 'guttae' in architecture, which is not particularly useful in real life since nearly all of us don't know what it means without looking it up. I only know about 'nycinasty' because I googled flowers seeming to shut down and go to bed at night but am glad such words exist.

Some time ago, there was a single wild yellow lupin bush teetering on the edge of the cliff, which I rescued and planted in our so-called garden, which I have subjected to a programme of 'managed rewilding' with a controlled let-it-grow policy in certain areas. The wild yellow lupin thrived and tiny baby yellow lupin plants popped up around its feet. Each of these was nurtured with the care of a mother hen nurturing her yellow chicks, with the result that now we have wild yellow lupins all over our part of the cliff, flowering in May and lasting for most of the summer.

The 'managed rewilding' also extended to the brambles, which were higher than my head and covered a large area amounting to about half the so-called garden when we were first here. By hand, with my parrot clippers, I chopped the brambles up into tiny pieces, which took several days. I left a thick hedge of high brambles at the boundary with the barley field behind us and behind the brick outbuilding, to act as cover for the songbirds, pheasants and hedgehogs I hoped might appreciate it and also to stop Chuffy running away into the wide blue yonder, as greyhounds are inclined to do.

Now, the former bramble patch is a carpet of blue flowers in May, a type of large forget-me-not, which must have been lying dormant in the soil, unable to see the sun or compete with the brambles. Essentially, I act as an intelligent grazing animal, strimming paths here and there, but leaving the wildflowers that I choose. I also allowed about twenty self-seeded tree saplings to grow into proper trees, cutting off the lower branches to channel their energy and make a good tree shape rather than a bush, in contrast to our high, bushy hedges left shaggy for the birds. After ten or so years, my pet saplings are now handsome young trees several metres tall, so it is startling to suddenly be reminded that they will end up in the sea before they reach the end of their natural life.

The effect of all this 'managed rewilding' on insect

life, and therefore bird life, is remarkable to observe. It has definitely made a difference and helped a tiny patch of nature. If I had done genuine hands-off rewilding and done nothing at all, rather than pretending to be an intelligent grazing animal, the benefits to nature overall would be (are) measurably less. We know this because we have the 'before' as a control to the experiment. Suffolk has been a cultivated landscape for so many centuries that it does not seem cut out for a return to the rewilding purists' Serengeti of woolly mammoths, wolves and lynxes that it once sustained, but with a 'Wilderness Reserve' of four thousand acres, nature reserves, estuaries, wetlands, abandoned wartime airfields, rough coastal edges and reedbeds, it still tries its best to be hospitable to wildlife.

In early spring, perhaps March or April so as to be in England for the blossom and cow parsley in May, we sometimes go to Venice. One such time, already knowing Venice well and having explored all the obvious places around the lagoon, from Torcello to Choggia, we alighted on the farming island of Sant'Erasmo, a large island that tourists almost never visit, just to see what it was like. Exactly like Suffolk, is what it was like. Apart from the farming of artichokes, whereas Suffolk goes rather more in for asparagus in that sort of high-value-crop arena, the watery landscapes of the Venetian lagoon and the Blyth estuary have much in common.

At the outer reaches of Sant'Erasmo, there was a bee-farmer selling honey and a chicken farmer selling eggs, on a small nature-friendly scale, reminiscent of Suffolk's thriving roadside honesty-box culture, of which we are quite proud (of the honesty as much as the enterprising spirit). There was also a mysterious dam made of branches and twigs, with some kind of trap on the bank of the dyke which was dammed. The dam looked man-made, and the trap was a small wire cage, of the sort possibly intended to catch some kind of mustolid predator, perhaps a mink or a stoat, that the Sant'Erasmans considered a threat to the local fish or water voles. But it seems unlikely that a mink or a stoat would ever have found its way to an island in the first place. I have no idea what the cage trap might have been for, but it was an incongruously rural scene to find in Venice.

Mysterious dark arts have always been part of country life, legally and illegally. There used to be a gruesome tree on an abandoned airfield near Metfield in Suffolk. The tree was hung like a Christmas tree with dead predators and 'vermin' of many kinds and I only saw it because I was on a horse, off-roading in that remote spot. If the mobile-phone-camera had been invented at the time, I might have taken a photograph, for historical posterity, and so that later generations could contemplate progress made in our relationship with native wildlife. The 'vermin tree' may still be there, like that. Moles are still hung along fences in some places, the traditional mole-catcher's 'invoice', so that he can be paid per mole but cannot present the same mole to another farmer and be paid twice. Old-school mole-catchers bemoan the lost art of mole-catching, which used to be done with a device made of horsehair and willow, instead of a skill-less modern trap. And modern sensibilities tend to condemn the word 'vermin' altogether, another almost-redundant rural word, like 'varmint'.

In a perfect world, wild animals would live happily into their old age surrounded by their grandchildren and cherished memories, like the old lady at the end of *Titanic*. The suffering of wild animals being naturally predated, injured or starved must be immense. In addition, since wounded or weak animals are the ones targeted by predators, evolution has taught these poor creatures to hide their suffering with stoicism, just to survive. On the plus side, you never see a fox or a stoat or a rabbit or a rat staring blankly out to sea with dementia.

Back to Sant'Erasmo impersonating Suffolk, nearby on the water was a flat-bottomed punt, of the kind used for wildfowling. Certainly, people in the Venetian lagoon go wildfowling and have done for centuries. There is a picture of a painting by Pietro Longhi (1701-1785), 'Hunting wild ducks with bows and arrows', depicting duck shooting in the *valli da pesca* in the Venetian lagoon, in my copy of *Francesco's Kitchen*, a book about the food of Venice by Francesco da Mosto. This painting is a reminder of the difficulty of the task our forbears faced catching their food, trying to shoot a moving small target with a bow and arrow from a wobbly boat, skilful as it still would be even with a gun. An article in *The Field* (Feb 2017) 'Just One Mallardo' (typical British Italiano which does no justice to the scholarly content) gives a detailed account of early-morning wildfowling for wigeon in Venice, including a potted history of wildfowling in the lagoon going back to 1268, when it was decreed that the Doge had to give ducks to the Great Council who had elected him. On the island of Mazzorbo there is a place called *Ai Cacciatori*, which offers local seafood and wild game on the menu when in season. *Cacciatori* being 'hunters'.

While tramping round Sant'Erasmo, I thought of how far our relationship with the catching of our food goes back, lost in the mists of time. Fishermen and wildfowlers must have been out at dawn and dusk in the Venetian lagoon and in the Blyth estuary, hoping to bag a fish or a duck for the pot, with bow and arrow, net, spear, rod or gun, for as long as we have been human.

We have much in common with the Venetians, as they too live at the mercy of the sea.

MAY

Food in season and local 'sea state' update

Veg
Asparagus season begins, broad beans, spinach, sorrel, elderflower

Game
Muntjac, legal all year round

Meat
Spring lamb

Fish
Spring lobster, haddock, prawns, salmon, trout
Mayfly hatchings in chalk streams, 'evening rise' hatchlings rise to surface for brown trout

Distance from cliff
22 metres

Change since last month
No change, either visually or in measured land loss

A Night on the Dune

These are the things I prize
And hold of dearest worth:
Light of sapphire skies,
Peace of the silent hills,
Shelter of forests, comfort of the grass
Music of birds, murmur of little rills,
Shadows of cloud that swiftly pass,
And, after showers,
The smell of flowers
And of the good brown earth.
And best of all, along the way, friendship and mirth.

God of the Open Air
Henry Van Dyke (1852-1933)

6

JUNE

In the early morning, when the scent is low, you can smell the line of a fox as surely as if you had been born a foxhound. It is a strange epiphany to have these nano-seconds of insight, momentarily to sense the world as the wild animals and our own half-wild dogs must sense it all the time, an ordinary hedgeline suddenly transformed into an overwhelming multi-sensory experience, a conduit of useful information. The beach must be an ongoing canine soap opera, every washed-up object a frenzied canine Twitter. The line of the early morning fox-scent is clear only for a fleeting moment, because smell is such an ephemeral, uncatchable sense that almost as soon as it is perceived, it melts away into the landscape.

This particular fox is a playful soul and on one occasion he, or she, played a kind of peek-a-boo hide-and-seek game round the scruffy little barn, actually a World War 2 radar station of some kind, which sits in ruined isolation half way up the farm track leading south.

The rural fox in general and this fox in particular, usually avoids human contact, easily scenting my presence from hundreds of paces away, so it is difficult not to read his deliberately interactive behaviour as the fox having fun, teasing me, almost playing. It might have been some kind of practice exercise for hunting his quarry and prey, but the fox seemed to actively enjoy the game. He could easily have run away, but instead he crept stealthily round the base of the little wartime barn, in the manner of a predator stalking his prey, while I crept round in the opposite direction to meet him. He looked me straight in the eye for at least ten seconds, almost with a twinkle, then scampered off, leaping over the tall grasses, in an attitude of triumph. I warm to this fox, even though I have gone to considerable architectural trouble to thwart his devices and desires to kill our chickens.

People always say that smell is the sense most evocative of memory and that hearing is the last sense to go in the hour of our death (although how the living can know this is another of life's mysteries). The smell of mown grass or hay is often cited as the scent cliché most evocative of childhood, even though traffic and warm tarmac and air-borne junk food smells must be components in the scent-scene of the collective memory now.

One of many strange things about cities is that the air smells of their food combined with their architecture: London smells of sausages and solid stone, Venice of *fritto misto* and wet walls, Barcelona of garlic and Gaudi. The smell of a city is not very noticeable when you live there all the time but becomes vastly exaggerated once you return to your rural roots, give up smoking and live on a sea-breezy clifftop for much of the time. The smells of London are overwhelming on first arrival after the clean air of the cliff, but here, the still small smells of the cliff are quite discernible too, if you train your senses to 'listen' for them. It is quite telling that we don't have an accurate word for the mental equivalent of humans actively listening, but for smells not sounds, as a dog scents the air. Sniffing is not quite it. Nor do we have a word for a smelltrack as distinct from a soundtrack. We can talk easily about the soundtrack to our lives and childhoods, but we neglect the smelltrack which is undoubtedly there.

Typically for a certain kind of Englishness in manners and mannerisms, as children we were somehow imperceptibly indoctrinated to call scent in a bottle 'scent', not perfume or fragrance, and to call smells in the air 'smells', not odours or aromas. The words used reflect attitudes to different kinds of smells: healthy, wholesome, real, shameless, natural. No euphemisms. No French. No Franglais. Our familiar smells were those of a typically threadbare English country life: mothballs and furniture polish, flowers and fires, cobwebs and crumpets, pony books and guinea pigs, all competing against a continual background hint of damp and dogs and cold air. As a child, I wanted to spray my bedroom with the combined scent of pony and stable and saddle soap and tack and I still believe someone could make an olfactory fortune from bottled *Eau de Poney pour les jeunes filles*.

The early days of summer seem to last forever on our cliff, as if a sunny seaside location can momentarily recapture the essence of 1976 in perpetuity. Faint sounds of children bucket-and-spading are carried on the air from the beach huts, visible in the far distance, yet a world away. In the spirit of trying to recapture a half-remembered or imagined magical sense of freedom and endless summer holidays, we sometimes create a little adventure and spend a night outside on the dune. Here, we can rediscover the elemental life: earth, air, fire and water, catching and cooking, the sound of the endless waves breaking on the beach and the infinity of the stars above us.

Rosemary bushes and tamarind trees thrive on our clifftop, lending it an unexpectedly Mediterranean air, an almost exotic hint of more glamorous locations and warmer climes. This effect is exaggerated and enhanced by the summer-evening sounds of crickets cricking merrily away all about us, filling the air with their chirruping and rendering this particular patch of Suffolk 'below the cicada line' as certainly as it is now within the 'cooking-with-garlic' and 'wine-producing' regions of the world. Whether these Mediterranean characteristics are due to post-war culinary cultural crossover, from Elizabeth David to Francesco da Mosto, and air travel, or by actual climate change, is unclear, but in the immediate moment, the combined warmth of the smells and sounds can transport us to an instant Suffolk approximation of Liguria.

The unofficial path along the clifftop towards the beach changes its position every year, because of the erosion. The path always seems to be the same, but it isn't, as it carves its way through the waist-high wild flowers which grow along the cliff edge. When the vulnerable last five metres or so of edge-land is left unploughed, the secret seeds, long-embedded in the earth from forgotten ancient seasons many decades ago, suddenly spring to life. Within less than a year, the unploughed land thrums with busy insects and the scents of a thousand different native plants. Romantic rural names familiar to our great-great-grandparents are dusted off: sea milkwort, dumpy centaury, common valerian, wild angelica, fools' parsley, frog orchid, hairy vetch, tufted vetch, bitter vetch. Yellow wild lupins spread and selfseed wherever they are left undisturbed, each tiny lupin plant becoming a large woody bush, and all of them descended from the tiny 'last lupin' I rescued from the edge of the cliff a few years ago. The entire cliff-edge becomes a poignant carpet of red poppies in June.

Each of these plants carries its own breezy scents and earthy smells. Even the relatively plain grasses are worth noticing. You could sketch a different type of grass seed head every day for a year, and from the grasses descends the farm's principle crop: barley for the Adnams brewery, a traditional variety with short stems to survive the coastal winds, and a beautiful name, Maris Otter. At times, the whole of Southwold smells of beer and brewing, but really it is the smell of our barley, our fields of gold, our Maris Otter, which fills the air.

At the end of the flowering and seeding process, I collect seeds from the more attractive of these 'weeds', creating an inherently tough and mixture of native wild flowers known as Farmers' Nightmare, an idea I attribute entirely to the late Dame Miriam Rothschild, of *Rothschild*

Collection of Fleas fame. *The Rothschild Collection of Fleas* is an obvious target for easy mirth, the lazy comedian's laughing stock, but it is also a genuinely great work of flea research and taxonomy, which I have had the honour of seeing in the flesh at the Linnaean Society, on the lefthand side of the entrance to the Royal Academy on Piccadilly. I first learnt of Farmers' Nightmare from a book about restoring natural biodiversity to the estate and garden at Highgrove. The book shows a picture of an elegant old lady sitting outside in a chic wooden chair, surrounded by a froth of head-height cow parsley and plant life which obliterates any clear view of the country house visible behind her. The caption reads, 'Dame Miriam Rothschild gave up gardening in the formal sense in the mid-1950s ...', and it describes her invention of, or introduction of, the idea of Farmers' Nightmare. I feel I owe it to her to honour her memory by continuing her weed-seeding work, so I do. Self-seeding flowers are an under-rated treasure of nature for gardeners.

Old tramlines left by the tractor's wheels on some previous arrangement of the cliff, from last year or the year before, are always still visible, giving the disconcerting appearance of the tractor having recently driven straight off the edge of the cliff. The tramlines are a very characteristic feature of the pragmatically undramatic East Anglian landscape but are so taken for granted that we hardly notice their architectural perspectives and vanishing points, their straight lines and parallel geometries drawn into our fields of vision at every turn. The tramlines are also a useful reference point, when trying to pin down the extent and direction of the erosion.

Without a photographic record, taken from the same spot with the same sight-line and layering one year over the next, it is difficult to quantify the extent of the loss of land. The supposed Hundred Years Line means little in real life, on the ground, especially as no one can remember the date from which the mythical Hundred Years was meant to date.

What is certain is that the farm has lost 250 acres of arable land and two cottages since World War 2. But even then, the erosion was a known factor and this land was bought relatively recently in the 1920s, from the Benacre estate, when one of the Gooch family, who still live at Benacre, needed to sell land or the family silver to pay some death duties. Wisely, the 1920s Gooch chose to sell some of the diminishing land at the sea-edge of the estate, although they too still lose many acres of arable land every year, just to the north of us. It was knowable even before Google that the church of St. Nicholas Easton Bavents fell into the sea just after 1666. Talk of compensation for losses caused by coastal erosion, even for the farm, let alone the various holiday-house owners who seem to have scented a windfall in the windblown space where their houses used to be, is an awkward subject, given our long-known history as a crumbling country, but it crops up from time to time, locally and nationally.

For our night on the dune, we walk through the wild flowers and along the path to the place known locally as The Low, where we can walk onto the beach itself. This is where the encircling reedbeds meet the beach. At the far end of the beach, in a secret cove near the broad and the Zeus Tree, where the otters have been seen and where the swans gather at dusk, there is a secret fire place. Hidden from view from the beach by a shallow dune and separated by some distance from any natural fuel except driftwood on the beach, it is safe from the risk of accidentally starting a wildfire through the reedbeds or the gorse, or the Scots Pines wood where the foxes and pheasants and muntjac live. From time to time there maybe roe deer and red deer passing through those woods as part of their wider territory, as well as the elusive white hart.

The driftwood for firewood that washes up on this beach tends to be broken-up offcuts, shards, blocks and planks from something constructed or formed by man, with a few very large pieces of our white-bleached fossilised trees like the Zeus Tree, and the occasional large piece of boat or building. There is little of the artistic natural silvery forms so beloved by coastal style magazines. I have built a table in what might be captioned 'shipwreck style'. From my everyday firewood-foraging observations, I can only presume we should be on a rougher and more vastly oceanic coast for that sort of driftwood. Perhaps there is an online shop from which people buy artistic silvery weather-worn driftwood, proper driftwood-that-actually-looks-like-driftwood, shipped from distant islands in the Pacific or the Caribbean, like the shells imported from far off shores, bought to fill glass jars in beach-themed bathrooms by the sea in Brighton or Bude. For many people, there seems to be a visceral yearning for the sea or for reminders of the sea, which speaks of ancestry and romance and race memory reaching far back along the centuries and our human timeline, while for others, the sea seems entirely absent from thought or need.

Before our night on the dune, we walk with Chuffy towards Benacre, to gather some firewood and see the local sights, such as they are. A little building has fallen off the cliff onto the beach. Its small size and pragmatic boxiness hints at some wartime functionality, but its position on the beach also hints at an unexpectedly dramatic erosion event. Normally, all our local buildings are dismantled before they notionally topple off the cliff. While slightly disconcerting in its immediately local unpredictability at times, the pattern of erosion along the east coast is essentially foreseeable. As with rising sea levels, we can plan for change, and we must. Churchillian rhetoric is no match for the mighty forces of nature we see at work in this gentle place.

Now to our driftwood beach-fire, where we add a few small brushwood offcuts from our overgrown rosemary and tamarind, lending the Suffolk wood smoke the earthy scent of our imagined Ligurian hills with a Mediterranean evening sun setting against the olive groves. The fire crackles and hisses and spits on contact with the oil in the rosemary stalks, investing our billy-kid goat-meat sausages with the earthy smells and flavours of an aromatic herbal incense. Sometimes we might cook a fish, a mackerel or a bass, or skate wings from the hut at the harbour. Today we are honouring the billy-kids. The spirit of Henry Beston and *The Outermost House* is revived in these moments, his words remembered: *'The world today is sick to its thin blood for lack of elemental things ... for fire before the hands ...'*

The immediacy of just *being* by the beach-fire is all-consuming: the charred wood shapes, the turning of the billy-kid sausages, the smoke, the rosemary-oil smells, the mythical animal-pictures leaping from the flames as ephemeral and ever-changing as creatures seen in passing clouds, the waves crashing on the shingle and sand, and the calls of distant creatures as they roost and have rows about who rules the roost tonight. Everything is in the present moment.

Out here, tending our fire, every sense is slightly alerted to some unknown animal danger, every sinew slightly more aware than usual that something might happen. Our nostrils twitch like those of a fox in search of fur or feather, or Chuffy in search of a billy-kid sausage. Our ears our pricked for the slightest sound: the crack of a hoof on a twig in the woods, an owl, a shipwreck, smugglers, people-traffickers, the faint possibility of some distant fisherman's scrunching footsteps as he settles down for a lamp-lit night after the bass. But, tonight there is total silence. We are alone. We are wild animals at dusk.

I pick up a twig of rosemary, holding the end where the bright young leaves of new growth are, and then run the other hand backwards along the twig, against the grain of the older dark leaves, so my hands smell of rosemary. The old rosemary needles flare up in flames for a second, as they land in the fire. I thread the resulting bare rosemary twig through the first of the smoky billy-kid sausages and hand it to Giles, a primitive gesture I like to imagine is comparable to the intense sensual intimacy of a man lighting a woman's cigarette in a black-and-white film. The rosemary sticks are a practical way of not burning our hands, a rustic interpretation of the kebab skewer or cocktail stick. Chuffy will not be left out of our rustic camp-fire feast. He will sleep outside with us and be our guard dog.

For a night on the dune we need no camping kit, no cutlery, no tent, no rucksack, no map, no whistling kettle, no nothing. Just an old wool rug and the billy-kid sausages and the rosemary twigs. If a freak wave were to wash us away now, all that would remain of us would be the tiny buttons on our shirts, which are probably not mother-of-pearl, although they might be, and perhaps the soles of our sun-bleached canvas shoes (of the sort which used to be called 'sand shoes'), which might not be made of actual natural rubber. Everything else is bio-degradable, wool or cotton or wood or rosemary twig, or us. The billy-kid sausages were wrapped in grease-proof paper, which long ago turned to dust and ashes in the rosemary-scented beach-fire before us.

As the fire fades, I use a stick as a poker to arrange the warm ashes and sand to extinguish the last of the faint glow, although the scent of rosemary still fills the air. The darkness sharpens the sense of smell as the night sky opens up above us, and the Milky Way begins to be visible between the most obvious stars, as our eyes adjust to the black night. We still have properly dark skies on this cliff. There is very little light pollution at the Easternmost House, despite our relative proximity to civilisation and to a working lighthouse, at the edge of this beautiful but densely-populated small island.

The only light visible from beside our beach-fire is an occasional tiny dot from an oil tanker far out to sea, so far away as to be almost imaginary, and the International Space Station. The International Space Station appears as if a bright star, passing from right to left across our sky at predictable times and all carefully mapped out on the internet. It passes directly over us in phases of a few consecutive days at a time, for about three minutes each time, about once every hour and a half, just after it passes over the Amazon rainforest and then Morocco and before it heads out on its way towards Kazakhstan or thereabouts, orbit-route-wise.

The smells of Earth must be overwhelming for astronauts when they return after six months in the International Space Station, a paradoxically confined and sensually-deprived bubble, on the edge of infinite of space. But we are also on the edge of infinite space. Wherever we are on Earth, it is odd to reflect that each one of us is at the geometrically-perfect centre of our own individual sphere: a dot at the centre of a circle in plan, a dot at the top of a circle in section or elevation, each at our own personal North Pole, with the whole of our planet spread out evenly beneath our feet, even though much of the time we must appear by conventional orientation of the school-room globe to be 'at a funny angle' or 'upside down'. My own tiny globe, a blue and green glass marble barely 20mm in diameter, is always a useful tool for seeing life from a different perspective.

We adjust ourselves to our night on the dune. Chuffy has already searched his bed for snakes with his feet, turned a few precautionary circles and curled himself up for the night in a cosy dip in the sand. I secretly tie him to me on a long lead so he can't lope off into the night and do mischief, as greyhounds sometimes do when they feel the blood of their ancestors stirring and hear the call of the wild. Gamekeepers tend to go green at the gills at the sight of a longdog near their pheasants. We lie out on the dune, in silence under the vast universe, as the waves shush us to a state of half-watchful near-sleep, then just the waves and breathing, and then sleep itself.

We will be woken by the dawn chorus and the sunrise. If we are lucky, we may hear the boom of the bittern in the reedbeds. Sometimes seals sunbathe on the beach in the early morning, but more usually there is a familiar consortium of characters from *The Ladybird Book of Sea and Estuary Bird*s, swans and murmuring geese on the broad, mallards quacking comically as they fly in to land, sand martins flitting in and out of their holes at the top of the crumbling cliff, sanderlings tottering about on the shoreline, unseen curlews, oyster catchers and terns nesting on the shingle and a few lone herring gulls gliding along the line of the cliff.

Since we constructed nest boxes, insect hotels and feeding stations in its untidy wilderness areas, our garden has become a haven for reed buntings and other songbirds. Skylarks practise aerobatics, far up in the sky over the rippling barley fields, as their song fills the air. The sun arrives with us before it arrives anywhere else in

England, or in Britain, and it will warm the earth along the cliff where it faces the rising sun, so that the scents of wild flowers will reach us long before any hint of the smell of strong coffee.

Home-made Pimm's

June, the month of early dawns and sunrise-watching at '0434hrs' on the beach. The Derby, which would have been The Bunbury, after a Suffolk family, if a bet had gone the other way. Royal Ascot. Rural cricket. Peak honesty-box asparagus at the Sea Breeze asparagus farm just up the road at Benacre. The season of elderflower cordial and home-made Pimm's. The longest day. The easiest month. Summer, but before all the visitors arrive.

You'd think it would be easy enough to become a hermit living somewhere like the Easternmost House, stuck out here on the edge of the cliff, but it's not. The paradox is that it is easier to be anonymous, or a recluse, in the city. In addition to lack of anonymity, it often seems impossible to work on a 'proper job' for any sustained amount of time, such as every single weekday for several weeks, without being interrupted by some rural crisis or a request for participation. This is not because of a decline in agriculture, or viticulture, or horticulture, or any other kind of culture (including rural architecture), nor is it the result of there not being enough to do. It is because in this part of our crumbling country, we have so many parties and events in aid of good causes.

There is a yearly cycle as predictable as the tides and

seasons: cricket matches, garden open days, horse shows, dog shows, horse-and-dog shows, hunter trials, snowdrop walk days, daffodil days and then full circle back to cricket matches, all in aid of genuinely worthy causes. And that's before you start on the farming calendar, or the church calendar, or your own normal life. By the time we've been roped in to help organise these events, and been food shopping for them, and cooked for them, and moved all the furniture around, and been to the party, and cleared up afterwards, and then been to the bottle bank, there is hardly any time left to do proper work at all.

Luckily, June heralds the summer solstice, the fabled Longest Day, which is badly needed, just to catch up on all the lost time. This pattern is repeated in any rural area in Britain, largely unknown by any visitors who might happen to be driving through the landscape, just as the larks at dawn and the hares at dusk are unseen by the passing car.

At one such fund-raising event this year, the host had kindly donated fourteen lambs, who had until recently grazed and decorated the partying land, and now joined the party on a plate. Bach was wrong. Sheep may not safely graze. But the noble lambs had a good life and contributed to the life of the landscape which sustained them.

Interspersing these actual events, many evenings are spent at meetings, constructing and deconstructing, and counting the money. Post mortems are essential for trying to avoid the same disasters in subsequent years. We aim to have different disasters. Record-keeping about numbers is important too. Someone will complain how nobody replies to invitations properly. Someone else will complain about the modern blight of people asking *why* someone can't go to their whatever-it-is. Just as the great advantage of black tie is supposed to be that it is a social leveller, preventing sartorial embarrassment by introducing rules and certainty, so the great advantage of the old-fashioned, no-explanation, third person invitation reply, 'very much regrets . . . due to a previous engagement . . .', is that it makes it quite easy to say, 'I don't really want to go to your whatever-it-is, because I'd rather stay at home with my dog watching Wimbledon', without sounding incredibly rude.

The Dog Day started badly as the Burco Boiler whooshed and hissed in the corner like a steam locomotive rendered breathless from the chase. The monsoon prompted stoical mutterings. The pony fancy dress class was won by a fully-manned tank on operations in a war zone, the whole pony-and-child-unit draped in ex-army camouflage, with a turret and gun made of cardboard boxes and tubes. On it goes, year after year, these peculiar and apparently quaint vignettes, constantly evolving to adapt to modern rural problems, keeping the roofs on churches stripped of their lead, reviving a tired shop, subsidising a remote pub, helping a depressed farmer, comforting a bereaved teenager, keeping the air ambulance in the sky.

The terrier racing is always exciting. Every terrier heat begins with the same frenzied scrabblings at the doors of the traps, gnashings of the teeth of terror, squealings in anticipation of the ratty lure . . . Kerchoong, off they go! Little legs whizzing along . . . trying to catch . . . up with ... that fluffy rat grrrr! Rat grrrr. Whizzing back the other way and back again. Missed it. Ratgrrr. Through the pop-hole in the straw bales at the finish. Ratgrrr. Grrr. GRRR. Fight, fight, fight! GRRR! FIGHT! A bit of a scrap at the end of each race. Aggressive little things, terriers. Terrierists. But the Air Ambulance may fly another vital sortie, aided by the small change raised from the little tykes' paltry entry fees.

The inevitably final item on the agenda, at least once a year, is the recipe for home-made Pimm's, for the forthcoming summer Pimm's party. We can't remember why we need to revisit the recipe every year. We can't even remember why we make our own Pimm's. It undoubtedly involves more palaver, but there is a certain exclusivity amongst fellow home-made-Pimm's-makers, a shared experience in the subtle tracking down of the elusive, crucial ingredient*. The recipe is as follows:

> Home-made Pimm's
> Gin (40% proof): One unit
> Red Vermouth: One unit
> *Orange Curacao: Half a unit
> The units can be anything, because it's 2:1 ratio
> by volume.
> We mix it 1:4-ish with diet lemonade, to avoid
> excessive sweetness.

This year, we will order the orange curacao specially, because it is now so rare. Mr Carr at the wine shop in Halesworth, who is very supportive of rural causes, will provide. This is important. We must have a very efficient summer Pimm's party this time, to make up for last year and the Affair of the Green Pimm's.

At the summer Pimm's party last year, we mixed our gin and vermouth, and then added our curacao in the correct proportion, as per the instructions. So, imagine our curious surprise when a vibrant green liquid appeared. Visually, we had created a dead-ringer for Fairy Liquid. What could we do but proffer this strange cocktail to our guests with airy confidence and hostly aplomb? So that is what we did. The lemonade diluted the colour, but only marginally and at aesthetic cost, adding Fairy Liquid-y bubbles to the mix. The borage looked pretty, but the mint gave misleading visual cues in the context of that lurid green hue.

Three people described on the invitation as 'musicians' sat in a dilapidated little white tennis hut, a rumbunkle structure lurching at the edge of the lawn, playing screechy summery tunes on their primary-school-style recorders, in the gathering sea-fret, albeit a few miles inland on this occasion, but well within the wider territory of the Easternmost House. The combination of all these individually unpleasant factors conspired to create a somewhat elemental party atmosphere. Guests meandered about among the croquet hoops, adjacent to a green-fuzzy expanse of cracked tarmac, the tennis court.

It was a typically English summer scene: summer dresses and flower-garden colours, panama hats and floppy linen, mucky old coats hastily scrambled from cars to fend off the unforeseen sea-fret, against a backdrop of an attractively crumbling country house setting. How lovely, at least in theory. If someone had constructed such a spectacle for a film, they would be accused of cliché and exaggeration, of cynically appealing to the dollar by fuelling the already widespread perception in that this is how all English people live, all the time. Yet there we all were, in real life. The possibility of moving this bedraggled cast of non-film-stars into the house was never mentioned. It crossed my mind that we might raise more money for the cause if the sporting punters were invited to pay *not* to endure such stoically jolly experiences in the future. But country people are of necessity a sociable and resilient tribe.

No one looked surprised by the greenness of the mystery cocktail. No one said anything rude about it. No one complained. No one even asked what it was supposed to be. They just chatted and drank their Fairy Liquid, and laughed, and ate their mini Yorkshire puddings with roast beef and horseradish, and crunched their way through quails' eggs with their shells still welded on (apparently, we should have peeled them while still hot) as if there was nothing remotely unusual or eccentric about drinking green Pimm's in a recorder-accompanied sea-fret. We learnt our lesson. Gin, red vermouth and *blue* curacao does *not* make home-made Pimm's.

The Easternmost House's elderflowers are in full bloom, bursting romantically through the ruined farm buildings at the far end of the track, so I must strike while the iron is hot and make some elderflower cordial for another fund-raising summer Pimm's party. It doesn't really matter what the specific cause being fund-raised for is or was, as there is always a need for what I call 'unprofessional catering'. We have people to lunch, people to stay, people to pacify and people to please. Home-made elderflower cordial is the rural elixir that oils the wheels of all these scenarios.

After the infamous blue/orange curacao mix-up with the home-made Pimm's, still referred to by some as the Affair of the Green Pimm's, people may be extra-cautious and go for the safe elderflower option this time. It is therefore imperative that I make the elderflower cordial correctly. The only thing I know about making elderflower cordial is that the professionals at Belvoir Castle put citric acid in it. Everyone round here, except me, will know the proper method, so it should be easy. I have to go to Halesworth anyway, to order the elusive orange curacao for the home-made Pimm's, so I shall buy some citric acid and get the whole operation out of the way today. Job done.

Later

What an amazing little town Halesworth is. On the very rare occasions when we seek something it doesn't sell, it performs its special trick. After I ordered the orange curacao from Mr Carr, my quest for citric acid began . . .

The obvious place to start is the chemist, but it turns out that there has been a run on citric acid because of the elderflowers being in full bloom. There's a surprise. One lady tried to buy the last eight packets this morning, but she wasn't allowed to because of the drug addicts. Eh? Did I know that in Italy the *drogati* use real lemons,

Slow Food-style, for something to do with their drugs, and they block public loos with all their lemons? No, I did not know that, but I do now. Thanks. You'd think the chemist in a rural market town such as Halesworth would have had the foresight to prepare for the elder-flower season and order citric acid in bulk. It is exactly the same attitude to shopkeeping that results in a dearth of orphan lamb formula milk at lambing time. Efficient shopkeepers in London would never run out of orphan lamb formula at lambing time, if they sold it.

As last year, I again resolve to stockpile citric acid when-ever I find it, but I always forget, just like the shopkeepers. The next most obvious place to look for citric acid is the Focus Organic shop. They are very healthy in this shop, selling worthy food and nettle shampoo, which I can only presume must be aimed at incomers and people down from London. I can't imagine real country people liking the idea of nettle shampoo, although it is certainly a possible busi-ness opportunity to expand the nettle range. My instinct is that if nettles were really any good for anything, we would be farming them already. I head for the pigeon holes full of little packets of weighed-out herbs and spices in eco-friendly minimal packaging. The pigeon hole marked 'citric acid' is the only one in the rack which is little-packet-free. They have 'runned out' (as we say in Suffolk).

A heavily pregnant and young-looking girl, a fellow customer with foal at foot in the form of a toddler, informs me that there has been a run on citric acid, and don't I realise that it is the elderflower season, and that the elderflower is flowering? I thank her for this insight.

This little vignette reminds me of a scene in *Cold Comfort Farm*. I half expect her to tell me that, 'Every year, in the fullness o' summer, when the sukebind hangs heavy from the wains . . . 'tes the same. 'Tes the hand of Nature, and we women cannot escape it.'

Feeling vaguely relieved that I am not youthfully pregnant, my eye is drawn to the fascinatingly realistic hyper-modern farm machinery grandly on display in the toy shop window, a far cry from our toxic lead hunting scene, but out of the same Britain's model-farm stable and at the same scale. There are no nostalgic and chaotic little Ladybird Book farmsteads in this educational arena. Suffolk's baby farmers are clearly being primed for intensive agriculture on a grand scale. Vast agro-chemical sprayers with all associated appendages await the eager under-fives. The Prince of Wales and Lady Eve Balfour would be in despair at the sight of this appallingly non-organic paraphernalia, aimed as it is at ones so young.

The greengrocer's shop wafts a breezy smell of fresh fruit 'n' veg. You would never have thought fruit and veg could smell so appealing. I buy masses of lemons but would feel better with some proper citric acid as well. Mr Palmer sells me some prize-winning free-range Blythburgh pork, with dog mince made from the squeamish bits. Next door, we discuss ways to cook squid and marvel at the weirdness of cephalopod anatomy. Nolly at the pet shop says you don't need citric acid at all, the sugar is a preservative, and here are Chuffy's pig's ears, two for a pound, thank you very much. Simon, the mynah bird, says, 'Hello. How *are* you? Quack, quack', as he always does. Everything but citric acid. Halesworth has failed me. This is unheard of.

There is no citric acid at the Adshop, the photocopy shop, where my drawings are printed, but they have some superlative stationery, as in 'the sharpest scissors in Suffolk', 'the stickiest sellotape in Suffolk', etc. The Adshop is possibly the only photocopy shop in the world where customers are given gigantic free courgettes with their photocopies during the courgette-glut season. Some of the fecund courgettes are like sleek, plump, green dachshunds, which have hidden under the leaves for five days, unnoticed, expanding, enormous.

I then have a brainwave and go to the bookshop, where I plan to do some sneaky 'browsing' in the book of choice. Although I have a copy at home, I need the information now, so I discreetly look up elderflower cordial in Hugh Fearnley-Whittingstall's *River Cottage Cookbook*, on the off-chance that he might say that citric acid is not absolutely necessary. Hugh lets me down. Although his recipe includes the extremely useful word 'optional', and he confuses the issue by calling it tartaric acid, I conclude that it must be a little bit necessary or Hugh would never have mentioned it. Hugh is not one for fussiness. Hugh would certainly have eaten mud and mould all through his childhood, and still does I should think. I thank Peter The Bookshop Man, and try to look as if I will return very soon to actually buy one of his books. Which in fact I will.

It is neither early-closing day nor lunchtime (during which everything in Halesworth is 'Closed 1pm-2pm'), so I venture down Chediston Street, which leads me in a direction in which I never seem to go, just in case of success. It is possible that Halesworth will magically produce a secret shop I don't know about. It seems unlikely, considering that I have known this little town since the Co-op was a livestock market; since the dark ages of the Space Hopper Age when lorries still thundered through the Thoroughfare on their way to the A12, brushing against terrified pedestrians' hair, leaving people spatchcocked against the walls, palms flat against the trembling brickwork. Those were the days.

But, Halesworth being Halesworth, anything is possible and it does magically produce a secret shop. I spy a jumble of things on the pavement, some old and some new, and a sign adorned with a painted Union Jack: The Glory Hole. And very glorious it is too. The Glory Hole is the sort of shop I imagine might have seemed quite old-fashioned even in the 1950s. It sells old buttons, collections of egg cups, enamel plates and mugs, plastic farm animals, balls of wool; anything, as opposed to everything, in fact. All its wares are a mixture of old and new, meticulously organised into drawers and shelves and glass-fronted cabinets, by size, type, colour, etc. The taxonomists of The Linnaean Society would be beside themselves at this systematic arrangement of old eggcups by genus, species and sub-species. It is a tidy-minded person's dream. But The Glory Hole does not seem to sell citric-or-tartaric acid.

I am just exclaiming to the cheerful woman who runs it that I think she has a wonderful shop and that I will return when I can think exactly which type of old thing it is I need, when it dawns on me that she is precisely the sort of person who would know how to make elderflower cordial properly.

We engage in a discussion of various recipes and methods and I explain my citric acid predicament to her, tactfully omitting any criticism of the relevant shops. She shuffles through the door open to the sunshine at the back of the shop, muttering something about Steradent. Ye Gods! I hope she doesn't expect me to put Steradent in a large batch of elderflower cordial destined for public consumption.

When she returns, she explains that she bought some citric acid for the purposes of cleaning some metallic object or other, but then she soaked the thing in Steradent instead. She proffers a scientific-looking little white box on which I can only see the word 'Monohydrate'. She hands it to me. It says 'Citric Acid Monohydrate BP' on it. The price label says 79p, so I give her a pound and thank her profusely. Once again, Halesworth has triumphed.

No wonder an article, describing Halesworth in detail but without naming it, once appeared in a serious national newspaper under the endearing title 'A Little Town Called Content' ... Aaah.

Elderflower Cordial
1 kettle-full of just-boiled water = 1.5 litres
= 2 wine bottles of cordial
Half a bucket of elderflowers
I normal bag of white sugar
3 or 4 lemons, juice and zest
1 normal little box packet of citric acid

Put all the water and ingredients in a big preserving pan or similar and stir to dissolve the sugar. Cover and leave in a cool, dark place, stirring two or three times a day, for about five days. Bottle into sterilised, or at least hot-washed, screw-top wine bottles, which look and feel nice to use. Bottle into plastic bottles, with space left for expansion at the top if intending to freeze it.

Post Script

Since the point of *the Easternmost House* (the book, not the house) is partly to evoke a sense of place, and partly to preserve for posterity the essence of a time and place that will soon be lost to erosion, and to the natural forces of progress, here I must add a post script to this episode.

One day, a bunch of flowers appeared in the place normally inhabited by Simon the mynah bird, behind one of the elegant sash windows of what was Nolly's Pet Shop. A little notice informed us that 'Simon passed away peaceful last night or early morning'. There was a little piece mourning the demise of Simon in the *East Anglian Daily Times* and a photo of Simon with Nolly. Cards began arriving at the pet shop, until Simon's window became a miniature shrine to The People's Mynah Bird. It was all rather sweet really, just about staying on the right side of mawkish. Halesworth had certainly lost a significant character. Simon seemed to enjoy his life conversing realistically with the people in the Market Place, and twenty-two is generally considered to be a good age for a mynah bird.

As is the way with coastal erosion, changes and losses in wider rural life can come hard and unexpectedly, after long periods of relative stability. Shortly after the death of Simon the Mynah Bird came the death of Nolly's Pet Shop itself, shortly followed by the closing of the The Glory Hole and then the Adshop.

More recently there was a devastating fire at Patrick's, the last remaining newsagents, delivering to all the villages. The only consolation was that the parrot was saved, the successor to Simon the Mynah Bird.

These cataclysmic losses were the rural business equivalent of a major cliff fall at Easton Bavents after a violent storm. Such change seems to come from nature as if nothing can stop it, but the memory of the place as it was still exists in local memory. Just as it will when our cliff goes.

JUNE

Food in season and local 'sea state' update

Veg
Asparagus, courgettes, green beans, salad, artichokes, mangetouts

Fruit
Strawberries, raspberries, gooseberries, cherries, elderflower cordial-making season

Game
Muntjac

Fish
Lobster, crab, prawns, whitebait, hake, salmon, trout

Distance from cliff
22 metres

Change since last month
No change

Summer Lightning

Eternal Father, strong to save,
Whose arm hath bound the restless wave,
Who bidd'st the mighty ocean deep
Its own appointed limits keep:
O hear us when we cry to Thee
For those in peril on the sea.

William Whiting
Hymn, written 1860, after Psalm 107

7

JULY

The Suffolk coast surrounding our cliff is a gentle, benevolent landscape with a temperate, undramatic climate. We have no lofty mountains and we experience no hurricane seasons or monsoons. It looks pretty, but this place is deceptively dangerous. People drown on their summer holidays. Small sailing boats can be caught out surprisingly close to the shore. Swimmers are swept off their feet by the undertow. Dogs and children are no match for the strong currents. Walkers on the beach can be stranded by the rising sea. The estuary will quickly becalm you on lethal mudflats if you neglect to study the navigable routes and tide tables. This is a not a landscape that is out to get you, but it will if you don't #respectthewater, as the RNLI constantly reminds people to do. Sometimes, the mighty forces of nature are just too vast and the lie of the land too low. The 'mighty ocean deep' simply cannot 'its own appointed limits keep'. It has happened before, and it will happen again. Sooner or later, the whole place will have to adapt to rising sea levels or be lost.

On the night of 31st January 1953, a fatal combination

of spring tides, a deep depression in the North Sea, wind, waves, unsophisticated forecasting and an inability to warn people, caused a storm surge which led to catastrophic flooding all along the east coast of Britain, with inevitable loss of life. It was Britain's greatest peacetime disaster, then. Lincolnshire, Norfolk, Suffolk and Essex were particularly vulnerable and 307 people died in these counties combined, including three in Southwold. This coast and its people are resilient and well-adapted to flooding. The Harbour Inn describes itself as 'beside and sometimes *in*, the River Blyth at Southwold Harbour', and calmly copes with the inconvenience of occasional tidal flooding, despite all practical precautions. But sometimes the sheer volume of water is simply overwhelming. A sign painted with '1953 flood level' hangs well above our heads on the front of the Harbour Inn.

In 2013, the 60th anniversary of the 1953 flood was marked in Southwold with a service of remembrance in St. Edmund's church. People who had been there recounted their experiences. As the wind whipped up and something rattled outside the church, one person began her story with a remark about how similar the weather had been early on that fateful evening had been, as it was today, now. It began as a normal windy storm.

We huddled together in the large church and listened to frightening stories about the sea ripping through Southwold Pier, ponies being rescued from the marshes and the tragic little tale of the baby in Ferry Road. You can still see where the deluge broke through over the fragile wooden houses on Ferry Road. There is a gap, where the land is imperceptibly lower, where those poor little houses used to be, and on whose plots no houses have ever been rebuilt. The spirit of Ferry Road is still intact, with some of the old wooden houses unchanged, so one can easily imagine the effects of the sea essentially breaking over them and onwards onto the marsh. Thousands of farm animals also perished in the floods.

One of the stories told that night in the church was a remarkable tale of coincidence, involving a boat belonging to a long-established local fishing family called Upcraft. Their fishing boat had been washed out to sea in 1953 and was lost. Since then, a generation of two Upcrafts had replaced the lost boat and continued fishing out of Southwold Harbour, dropping their nets and fishing the same area of North Sea for the sixty years since the flood. One day, one Upcraft caught in his net the actual nameplate from his family's lost boat. We thought about this as we sat in the church as the wind raged outside, and we marvelled at the unlikeliness of it, until I had the unwelcome thought that perhaps if one fishes the same small area of a shallow part of the sea, virtually every day for sixty years, it is not actually that unlikely that you might happen to catch your grandfather's old boat's nameplate in your net. Anyway, we all agreed that it was the most uplifting of the 1953 flood stories. The cherished nameplate now lives in The Sailors' Reading Room. The 1953 flood is very much alive in the local collective memory, even among those of us who were still a long way off being born when it happened. And it still has the power to cast fear over this coast and its people.

Although we are used to living in close proximity to the natural world, and quite accustomed to wild weather and coastal erosion, a storm surge poses a real threat. In 2007, we listened to the news on Radio 4, which told of storm surge warnings along the east coast. How interesting, we thought. That's us. Better watch out, etc. Radio 4 then advised us to tune in to our local radio station for information. It suddenly felt like some wartime public service announcement from an old Pathé newsreel. There was a palpable sense of genuine impending disaster, a real fear that sea conditions might rival those of 1953, that the sea walls and crumbling cliffs would be no match for what was to come. However much better warned we are now than the innocently ignorant people in 1953, a storm surge of that magnitude would still be a terrifying and dangerous event.

We listened late into the night as the tide rose, with high tide forecast at about 1.30am, or 0130hrs as the army would say, if they were here to help us. People battened down the hatches and looked at maps, trying to imagine what routes a large mass of water would take. Tension mounted. Lowestoft, Kessingland, Southwold, Thorpeness and Aldeburgh were deemed to be at most obvious immediate risk, but then it transpired that towns and villages further inland were directly in the path and immediately vulnerable if rivers such as the Yox and Blyth were to overflow. The clues were in the names: Yoxford, Eastbridge, Blythburgh, Blyford, Wangford. The tide rose and rose, and then it peaked and people held their breath, and the tide itself seemed to hold its breath, then just in the nick of time, it receded. Damage was certainly done in the storm surge of 2007 and some people suffered loss and inconvenience, but for those with 1953 in their mind's eye, it was generally considered to have been a mercifully narrow escape.

Up on our cliff, we have seen many passing storms: wild spray-flinging storms, foaming storms, petty little storms, sea-fret storms, storms where the sea appears to be level with the top of the cliff, dark storms, thunder-and-lightning storms, and storms that are like a complete rendition of Benjamin Britten's *Four Sea Interlude*s, performed by the actual seascape which inspired it, the music conjuring the mood of waves breaking on an empty shingle beach, eerie light, vast skies, fear of the unknown, people lost, an ever-present threat, an enormous natural presence, endless rhythms, continuous noise. But some storms are more memorable than others.

One night in high summer, we witnessed from an upstairs window an extraordinary one-off show of summer lightning. Just as I have once, but only once, seen a football-sized knot of snakes, and once, but only once, seen millions of button mushrooms spring up overnight around the edges of the old commercial apple orchards, and once, but only once, seen a freak crop of poppies take over a one-hundred-acre field of wheat, so, once, but only once, we have seen horizontal lightning lighting up the sea and the night sky as if it were broad daylight, only more so.

The summer lightning storm to end all others was in July, at about two o'clock in the morning. It began with thunder, then really loud thunder, so loud it was almost frightening, just because it was so unusual in its tone and mood. It fought with all the normal past experiences of thunder we had had and heightened our animal instincts to be extra alert and wary in some unspecified way, even though rationally we knew it was only thunder.

Chuffy woke up too, although he was not frightened of thunder, having lived outside in a racing kennel for so long, with no anxious humans to spark reciprocal anxiety in dogs by saying disturbing, uncomfortable, nervous things like, 'There's a good boy, don't be frightened, it's only thunder, it won't hurt you . . .' and so on. There was the odd flash of sheet lightning too, which was worth staying up for and watching, if only for the dramatic effect as it lights up the sea, like the intense moonlight of a full moon over the sea.

Then suddenly, there was an almighty crack of thunder, like the end of the world and a simultaneous flash of lightning that filled the whole of our field of vision over the barley crop and the sea. It was how you would imagine a nuclear explosion to be if you were right underneath it, only more so. The thunder and bright lightning continued in this manner every twenty seconds or so, as we watched this unexpected *Greatest Show on Earth Summer Spectacular*, aghast. The ripening barley rippled in the gentle breeze and bright light like the sea, pale green, then brightest yellow when illuminated in the lightning, then back to a peculiar 'nuclear' pale green. It was mesmerising, but there was more.

As the thunder drifted off over the sea in the general direction of Knokke-le-Zoute, the lightning remained, but it had changed. Now in isolated silence, great horizontal linear sparks of white lightning streaked across our little sky, over the barley and over the sea, like the twitching horizontal lines drawn by heart monitors in the last throes of a fatal heart attack. The horizontal heart-attack lightning became brighter and brighter, but with no thunder at all. And throughout all this, there was never the faintest hint of rain.

Eventually, the whole storm drifted away to the south-east. The general drift of this part of the sea is to the south, part of an anti-clockwise force on the whole of the North Sea caused by the Earth's rotation. This is why the sand which has crumbled from our cliff often washes up in front of a little blue beach house called Mandalay, down by the harbour, or on the beach at Thorpeness. That memorably startling exhibition of summer lightning made it abundantly clear that the enormity and power of nature is completely out of our control.

The landscape has visibly changed since we have lived here. Where once there was a dune, now there is flat beach and a clear view of the pier in the distance. Where once there was the end of the reedbed where it met the beach, now there is a sandy bay from the night when the sea came in over the land. Where once there was the famously photogenic Benacre Tree, with its bleached-out branches standing up in the sea like an artistic hand, now there is no sign of it since it washed away. Where once we walked a hundred paces to the edge of the cliff, past two cottages and on to the land on the edge known as The Retreat, with its cabin and a white beach hut, now we are the ones on the edge. There used to be a pig living in an outbuilding up here on the edge. Houses, dogs, life, people. All that has gone in ten years.

I have considered buying all three of the houses at the sea-end of our track at various different times in the past, but the last time one of them came on the market, the reed-cutters who came out of the mist like rustic guardian angels put me off the idea for good, with their persuasive warnings that Benacre had lost sixteen metres in one tide and the likelihood that the erosion was accelerating. While the houses were romantic and fairly priced to reflect the erosion, like a short lease, none of them has lasted as long as I would have expected and planned for. The Easternmost House is co-owned by the farm. Its eventual loss will affect several people quite considerably, as it is the last of old Easton Bavents, the end of us living here and another loss of income for the farm, to add to the loss of land and barley crops.

Leather on Willow

Life *at* the Easternmost House inevitably includes life lived *from* the house, extending into its wider territory as well as in its immediate home purlieu of the farm, the beach and the Blyth Estuary. In an English summer, with the threat of thunderstorms imminent, thoughts naturally turn to playing cricket.

When people think of England, often what they are thinking of is a version of rural England. The landscape plotted and pieced, the church steeple cutting the skyline, the village nestling in the valley, farmhouse and field, wildlife and woodland. Any rural view of England (and most in the rest of Britain) generally consists of some combination of the four cornerstones of rural life: farming, field sports, village and church, the whole overlaid with the native and migrant wildlife. A look at any 'Beautiful Britain' calendar generally confirms this: coastline counts as farming (fish); a grand country house counts as all four, vast rugged mountain and moorland scenes count as farming plus field sports and so on. Images of the British countryside were used to boost soldiers' morale, particularly in the First World War, with a sense of 'This is what we are fighting for'.

Events such as the annual cricket matches at the Old Rectory (the Old Rec of my childhood) tacitly support all four of these cornerstones at the same time, since the players and spectators may include farmers, fishermen, shepherds, gunsmiths, gamekeepers, wildfowlers, livery yard owners and possibly a few poachers, alongside estate agents, accountants and solicitors. It is a broad church and broadly assembled in support of the church. If it wasn't right there in front of us all for six days a year, it might seem from another age. Wikipedia, and an article in *The Guardian,* refers to this kind of thing as 'deep England', as if it were imagined and not real.

Picture the cricket match scene: the little grey flint church in the background, the pitch, the field in the foreground normally grazed by my mother's Jacob (spotty) sheep, now mown so closely that it now pulls off a bucolic impersonation of the Centre Court at Wimbledon, but with a few mole hills. The sheep, who have been helping to prepare this cricket pitch for months, are moved off the scene of their duty, so they watch with ovine interest from the other side of the old post-and-rails fence.

A green pony trailer, of the sort normally used for transporting Thelwell ponies, serves as the cricket-kit-storing pavilion. Little wonkily-painted number boards are strewn about on the grass beside it. The scoreboard is propped up on the nursery blackboard. The scorer arranges his trestle table and the book. Soon, he will ask for a pencil sharpener, as he always does. Somehow the pencil sharpener is never provided until he asks for it.

The umpire is flailing about like a drowning man in a Jacques Tati film, as he tries to put on his white coat. The white coat is provided by Mr Clevely, the poultry farmer, to lend gravitas to the umpire's decisions. A rugged open-sided tent and two flimsy garden-centre-ish 'gazebos' are assembled along the hedge-line, housing the commercial heart of the operation: the tea tent, barbecue and bar.

If you could now imagine retuning your ear to 'eaves-dropping mode', you will pick up fragments of utterances along the lines of, 'What a lovely setting', 'This is so English', 'I can't believe this is real', 'It's lovely that this sort of thing still actually happens', 'Sorry, I'm so late. I got completely lost . . .' and so on. The regulars say no such things, as it happens every year, but we usually try to pull in some new blood, hence the commentary. You are now as good as there in person.

So here we all are again. I have a filial duty to perform, helping. We are hosting the cricket match as one of many in the Saints' Festival of Cricket. The title is not an indication of the characters of the assembled people, but of the names of the scattered collection of villages taking part, all named after saints and collectively known as The Saints. On one map, which explained Suffolk in relation to farming, tourism and second homers, The Saints area was marked, 'They shoot burglars here'. Here be dragons, bow and arrow country, or Bermuda Triangle, would also give a sense of the *genius loci*. In the war, it was a vital zone of airfields and land girls, still utterly confusing to outsiders. Tonight, none of The Saints is playing in the Saints' Festival of Cricket, and the postal address says we are in Norfolk even though we are physically in Suffolk. Typical Suffolk.

This evening, the Waveney Harriers will take on the NFU, which means that the hunt are playing the farmers. As some of the farmers also hunt, it can be quite confusing. The perfervid conflicts that one might encounter on Twitter between 'pros and antis' at the mention of the word 'hunt' still seem entirely absent from real rural life. It is impossible to extract that single thread from the tapestry, as one would have to rewind one's whole life, removing friends and relations, neighbours, farriers, print shop owners, builders and churchwardens, not to mention many of the paintings on the walls and books on the shelves of most of our houses, to entirely exorcise all reference to hunting or hounds from this particular patch of land and life. Many of these people would go to the point-to-point or the Suffolk Show, where hounds are intrinsically involved, historically and in person. Old men and teenagers who fish for bass from the beach under the Easternmost House cliff might also turn up at the cricket and vice versa.

The Cricket Festival is an annual event, but not an ancient one. It started about twenty-five years ago when the dreary village fêtes of our childhood finally dissolved through a combination of natural forces, diminishing public desire to throw horseshoes at a stick and not raising enough money to pay the church quota (officially the 'parish share'). Health and Safety bods also frightened us by describing the liabilities which could occur if we offered pony rides. Some might see the disappearance of those traditional village fêtes as a tragic loss, another vital chunk of our 'cultural cliff' metaphorically falling into the sea. But in reality, they were dire. We progressed to the 'mini Game Fair' to raise funds for the wretched quota, until my father came up with the idea of the cricket and it seems to have stuck.

The cricket-pitch church's saint, St. Margaret of Antioch, is the patron saint of peasants. How appropriate. As the population was decimated by the Black Death and somehow never replenished itself, each church must now be maintained by twenty-odd (or twenty odd) people. None of us wants to be part of the generation that allows any of the cornerstones of rural England to fall off the cliff, so we truck on, until it's not our turn any more.

The church and these cricket matches are far removed from any notions of religion itself. At the cricket, Belief, or genuine Faith, would be far too serious a subject to bring up in a tea tent conversation. Belief is of the utmost irrelevance in this context. We have a duty to support the church regardless. 'To everything there is a season, a time to reap and a time to sow'. 'That peace which the world cannot give'. 'Lighten our darkness'. 'We have erred and strayed from thy ways like lost sheep'. The language alone is worth saving. Words like 'Rogation' still have meaning here, surrounded by crops, in what is still referred to as a parish.

There is a long collective memory involved in this ritual: seven years of bumper crops; plagues of locusts; loaves and fishes; water into wine; a last supper. Lent, Ramadan, Divali. Feast and famine. Food is central to all religions, so the tea tent with its expert cake exhibitions seems an appropriate way to raise the necessary funds. We also run a bar and a barbecue all day, the cooking kit itself having evolved from a recycled tractor in the old days, to a proper modern barbecue made out of an oil drum. On the raffle-prize table, there are a few jars of home-made jam, with a sign saying, 'Better than Bon Mammon', in Suffolk Franglais. 'Bun Mammon' would accurately describe this cricket economy.

Realistically, unless all these tiny rural churches can become something useful, they will soon become romantic ruins, as surely as our vanished clifftop church of St. Nicholas at Easton Bavents has fallen into the sea.

JULY

Food in season and local 'sea state' update

Veg
Broad beans, peas, beans, cucumbers, lettuce, rocket, garlic

Fruit
Strawberries, raspberries, gooseberries, bilberries, blueberries

Game
Muntjac

Fish
Grilse (young salmon), plaice, best month for crabs, lobsters, prawns and shrimps, brown trout, wild salmon

Distance from cliff
22 metres

Change since last month
No change

To the Harbour at Sundown

Far and few, far and few,
Are the lands where the Jumblies live;
Their heads are green and their hands are blue,
And they went to sea in a sieve.

The Jumblies
Edward Lear (1812-1888)

8
AUGUST

At Sea

It is all very well living on the edge of a crumbling cliff and looking at the sea, living with the sea in all weathers, being beside the sea, but sooner or later you have to actually plunge into it, feel its spray lash across your face, have your heart nearly stopped by its freezing waves, or go out on it in a boat from which you cannot see the land. It is interesting to note that the real harbour people, fishermen and people who build boats, never swim in the sea. Our local harbour wisdom says that swimming in the North Sea is for people who do not maintain their boats properly.

There is a seasonal influx of visitors to our coastal territory, just as there is in Cornwall or Venice. Naturally, this creates many tasks for us to undertake, to cater for the visitors' needs. One such is for me to be skipper's mate on a bright orange fast RIB (rigid inflatable boat) called Coastal Voyager, operating out of a black-tarred harbour hut, and offering three quite different kinds of boat trips: the sea blast, the seal and wind farm trip and the river trip. The task of being mate involves a mixture of roping, knotting, steering; waterproofing and life-jacketing the visitors, radioing and watching out for hazards: spotting harbour porpoises, birds, swimmers, jet skis and so on. The small fly in this delightful seafaring ointment is that 'something might happen' to the skipper, in which case responsibility for the boat and its passengers suddenly passes to the mate. The sea blast is the most frequent everyday summer trip, operating to a strict timetable in half-hour slots, all day long, with the seal and wind farm trips and the river trips, being rather more complex to organise, each requiring an equation balancing variables such as the amount of fuel required in relation to number of seats filled versus number of sea blasts lost and, in particular, the tides. The seals live on a sand bank, which must have a tide low enough to expose the sand to ensure that the seals are all lying about decoratively upon it, while the river trips require a tide high enough not to become becalmed in the shallows or mudflats. The visitors naturally treat the boat hut like a London taxi rank and cannot understand that this is a business governed almost entirely by small subtleties within the phases of the moon.

Once the visitors are waterproofed and life-jacketed, we all clomp out along a boardwalk to the boat. Everyone lines up alongside, while the skipper, or the mate, assesses their relative weights, while trying not to look as if we are eyeing up livestock at the Suffolk Show, nor seeming to appear too weight-ist. We then seat everyone according to their weight, in an attempt to balance the boat. Some leap into the boat like gazelles. Others seem to struggle with the very concept of a 'boat', as it gently bobs up and down in the breeze as boats do, never quite still. Everyone is welcome, as long as they have signed the disclaimer saying they are neither pregnant nor likely to be slain by various serious medical conditions. All sorts of disabilities can be accommodated. We help them with their seatbelts and show them how to quick-release them. Then comes the safety talk. Every. Single. Time. Everyone ready? Then off we go.

'Southwold Harbour, Southwold Harbour, this is Coastal Voyager. Are we clear to go out to sea with fourteen people on board please, over?' It's Channel 12 on the VHF radio for the safe haven of the harbour and talking to our own local Harbour Master, Channel 16 when out to sea and potentially speaking to the national Coast Guard, with real sea traffic.

The boat-owner and principal skipper was for many years the senior helmsman of the Southwold Lifeboat and has sailed the Southern Ocean. Other skippers are similarly competent and at home on the sea. You'd need to be, with lives in your hands all day. The mate unties the mooring rope and attaches the kill-cord, which cuts the engines if the skipper falls overboard, and the boat trundles quietly out of its habitual hut-land home towards the harbour mouth and the open sea. People wave from the river bank. Then suddenly there is a thrust of power, comparable to the moment when an aeroplane switches from taxiing to actually taking off. And suddenly we're sea-blasting. The experience of being out at sea is so immediately and completely different from just looking at the sea that it can be slightly startling to those who are unused to it. Everything is wilder and noisier, wetter and windier, and we are always on the brink of being scared by the sea. We zoom around, up to the pier, out to the site of the Battle of Sole Bay in 1672, perhaps along the cliff to the north, where we can see our now-precarious-looking cottage and I talk about living with coastal erosion. Seen from a bobbing boat out at sea, our cottage looks quite adventurous and pioneering, even though I know that there is a Chuffy sleeping quietly in his bed, not being adventurous and pioneering at all. Chuffy, the snoozing greyhound poet-adventurer.

It seems inappropriate to describe a fast-RIB sea blast in words. It is very much an experience of the senses in the present moment. Being slammed and bounced across the waves, being cold and wet, or in T-shirts in glorious sun, or both at the same time, always, always makes you keenly aware that this is a moment on the edge of your normal safe life. To bounce across rough waves in a fragile piece of inflatable architecture is exhilarating, it makes you feel more alive, it engenders excitement, it stirs up the adrenalin, it enhances the senses with an enjoyable degree of latent fear, yet there is always the faint presence of the unwanted guest on the boat, the rogue wave, the unseen flotsam, the urgent radio voice rendered inaudible by the slamming of the wind and the waves, the risk, the sea, its unsayable possibilities.

Zooming around on the sea, with Southwold looking pretty and sweet, like a model village with its now-tiny-looking lighthouse and church and beach huts, makes people really happy. It is a constant joy to see their faces, to play a small part in making people feel this way, to give them future happy memories to draw on. We stop for a moment while I take the inevitable photos – here we are on a boat, with Southwold in the background – for their Twitters and Instagrams and Facebooks. Personally, I would ask everyone to drop all their phones into a bucket on the way out of the hut, all the better to live in the moment, to feel every second of bouncing through the waves and the spindrift, searing it into their minds forever, unrecorded. It is time to click the radio back to Channel 12 and call the Harbour Master, to see that the coast is clear for our return. People along the harbour wall wave every time Voyager returns. This tough, seaworthy, seriously powerful boat has quite improbably become as much a part of Southwold as the dinky little beach huts, indicating that even a place like Southwold is adaptable to change. Which is lucky. Southwold will certainly need to be adaptable, if the rising sea levels and coastal erosion forecast maps of the future turn out to be accurate. There is a harbour SOS group, Save our Southwold, but the stated aim is only to preserve the harbour for one generation. Beyond that, we can expect 'managed retreat'. This means that large parts of this land will be under water.

As we steer towards our landing stage, the next

boat-load of punters wait expectantly. We recognise some of the regulars, or types, who return every year: the whole family who turn up every summer dressed in wet suits, the estuary bird watchers, the hen party, the Italians, the excitable school trip, the twelve boys out for a twelfth birthday party, the families-who-holiday-together group, including the over-confident men who don't like being helped on with their life jackets, who like to make out that they habitually put on adventurous waterproofs, sail seriously and regularly, and are as at home on a rough sea as the skipper is, which they aren't.

The over-confident men are the ones to watch. They are the ones least likely to heed the RNLI's warning to #respectthewater. They won't have watched the RNLI's excellent #respectthewater survival-test film, because they thought they already knew how to survive. They think they are strong enough to swim to the shore, should they ever need to. It was an over-confident male windsurfer we found 'having a rest' on his board, half a mile off the pier. It was a group of over-confident men who thought they could just canoe up the estuary without knowing the river, without asking advice, without taking a map. They went straight on where the river bends sharply to the left, taking the most obvious and easy-looking route, but the wrong route. There is only one navigable channel and the rest of the estuary is a vast shallow body of water which becomes a mud flat at low tide. The over-confident canoe men became becalmed in mud and had to be rescued by Southwold Lifeboat. The over-confident men were in more danger than they realised and the lifeboat crew returned completely covered in black mud. That time, it was funny, afterwards. Other times have ended in tragic silence. The RNLI and the Southwold Lifeboat crew will tell you that more than half of the 160 people who accidentally die at the coast never intended to enter the water at all. They will try to explain that you should not try and swim against the tides and currents, that you should aim to be still and float with the current to conserve energy, to grab hold of something if the opportunity presents itself and not to panic. They will warn you that here, in our cold-water sea, hypothermia will probably kill you long before you drown, but if you survive long enough to get hypothermia you are doing well, because cold water shock in the first minute is the greatest danger of all. Cold water shock can literally stop your heart and produces a gasp reflex which may cause you to breathe in water not air. The RNLI will warn you that even if the lifeboat is immediately called out on a shout to come and rescue you, the chances are that by the time the heroic volunteer crew has assembled itself and the boat has been launched, you will have been in the water for at least ten minutes and probably more like twenty, which may be ten minutes too long. The RNLI will tell you to wear a life-jacket, but their rather obviously sensible advice still goes unheeded by too many too often too sadly. All summer long, we are the Jolly Roger, but in winter or in weather this can quickly become a different place, with an unbound river and a threatening sea. Even in August, you need to keep your wits about you. People, specifically visitors, seem oblivious of the dangers. They peer over the edge of our crumbling cliff, to see just how much it is crumbling. They go out to sea without radios or life-jackets. One sunny day, there were two children sitting on the wall right at the mouth of the harbour, where it actually projects into the North Sea. The lifeboat or any other boat would struggle to rescue them before the cold hit them. Swimmers don't take into account the undertow and strong currents, the raw trigonometry and geometry of how much further you have to swim and therefore how much longer you have to spend in dangerously cold water, when the distance to the shore is the diagonal of a rectangle, not the straight short side in their imaginations.

Each type of boat trip has its own character and mood. A typical sea blast is just half an hour of fun, like a roller-coaster ride but more elemental. People scream and laugh and get wet, and then it is over, a happy memory, a holiday treat. A seal and wind farm trip is necessarily less spontaneous, but more bonding. We take hot chocolate and we stop on the way back at the Yacht Club in Lowestoft. We are thrown together in conversation for a whole morning or afternoon. The seals conveniently live on a sand bank near the wind farm.

Possibly the greenest virtue of any offshore wind farm is hidden under the water line, where allegedly the concrete posts act like a wreck; it's as a haven for all sorts of sea- creatures, barnacles, crustaceans, crabs, lobsters and resulting fish eating the various smaller fish, which must also benefit the seals. Offshore wind farms are no-fishing zones, so the wind farm is an incidental watery wildlife sanctuary, an unwitting marine conservation area.

A seal and wind farm trip begins to feel like a genuine adventure, where individual personalities take on leadership or followership roles and you can begin to deduce who would survive or be most useful in an earthquake or a plane crash scenario, or more realistically who would be the heroes or the hopeless if terrorists struck again in London. Whenever there is a disaster, there are always calm people helping, straight away, with no warning. We can all secretly train ourselves to try and become one of those people, and arguably we should. We can mentally rehearse. We can think to ourselves, in advance, *if I hear a bang, assume it is a bomb, if I hear pop pop pop, assume first that it is gunfire, and act accordingly.* We can think, *help the wounded first, not the silent, don't be squeamish, rip up clothes as bandages and tourniquets, be firm even if it means having to be rough.* Being half a mile out to sea and five miles from the harbour, with strangers, with the potential for their lives and the safety of the boat to suddenly be your sole responsibility, focuses the mind on calm rehearsal for disaster.

The sea produces odd superstitions and altered perspectives. Part of the task of being mate involves pointing things out, telling people where we are and what they are looking at. As we passed Covehithe church, I said the word 'church' out loud, which triggered a sequence of reactions from the skipper, the upshot of which is that apparently it is unlucky to say the word 'church' out loud when out in a boat on the sea, ditto the word 'pig'. Or perhaps proper working harbour boat-people are just sharp on the teasing front and the alleged church-pig superstition was all nonsense.

From the sea, the Suffolk landscape offers a model of fashionable sustainability, with exactly the right proportions of land, water, trees, hedges, nuclear power stations, wind farms, fish, fowl and farm animals to sustain its low-density human population without needing any outside help. Suffolk could be cut off from the world and still survive, in perpetuity.

In a post-apocalyptic scenario such as a drone strike taking out the power supply for London, the evacuating urban population would be wise to head for Suffolk, the landscape still rich in resources and the people still sharp with the poaching, shooting, butchery and other 'rural skills' they would need to deploy to survive without our help.

The river trips are the sweetest and gentlest. The people who choose the river trips tend to be the calmest, the most interested in nature. The Southwold Harbour and what used to be called 'the navigation' was built by three local landowners, Blois, Rous and Barne, in the eighteenth century, to connect exportable crops from their farms with either the railway at Halesworth, or the sea. Before the harbour mouth was built, there had been a long sand spit causing an enforced detour every time anyone wanted to go out to sea. There are still Bloises, Rouses and Barnes living in the same places now, with the same farms and estates, albeit with a little shrewd selling and demolition having taken place on the country-house front in the latter half of the twentieth century.

On the marshes between the town and the river, there used to be a sea-salt-processing business, with its timber wigwam-like structure visible in some old etchings and engravings. Near the harbour mouth, where the Lifeboat Museum now is, there was a herring-smoking operation which took place in an attractive octagonal building known as the Kipperdrome. The small tower next to the landmark water tower on the common used to be a windmill. There are two more old windmills on the marshes, now treated as picturesque follies, but once crucial to a sophisticated system of pumping and manipulation of the water levels. Taking the long view, our ancestors have dealt with the same problems as we face now and resolved them in similar ways. The Dutch helped us control and manage our fenland and flatland water for several centuries and we may be wise to turn to them again. The eighteenth-century Dutch taught us how to make frameworks of willow and then use the ebb and flow of the tides to add earth infill to the frames to form solid, stable river banks, which are still here, largely intact. The river trips present an opportunity to revisit and explain a little of our past and to remind ourselves how and where and why these enterprises took place. We don't want to lose this knowledge. We may need it sooner than we think.

One little amusement on the river is to ask people what material a particular white boat is made of as we pass it. Much mumbling and discussion: can't be timber, too obvious, maybe fibreglass, plastic, steel, aluminium, recycled bottles, rubber, etc. The counter-intuitive answer is: concrete. Although in theory a concrete boat of the correct shape will float, this particular one sank and had to be salvaged. Concrete turns out not to be the ideal material with which to build your boat. The Brutalism school of architecture does not transfer successfully to the floating life.

All the way up the river, there are hundreds of different gulls and terns to see, nesting and congregating on the plentiful banks and islands, predator-free: herring gulls, common gulls, black-headed gulls, common terns, arctic terns, sandwich terns and little terns. The terns are wonderful fliers, floating and swooping gracefully above the boat, fishing in the river, gliding on the breeze. Swallows and swifts nest in the eaves of the boat hut every summer, and as the terns flit about the harbour with their forked tails like swallows, it is clear why they are also known as sea swallows. These balletic birds are an absolute delight, and it is so easy to take them for granted, to not notice them, to not really see them even though they are all about us.

Dorothy, the resident local pet wild seal, lives on an island at the far end of the estuary, on the last wide bend before the river approaches the White Hart pub in Blythburgh. She is a common seal, like most of the seals on the sand bank near the wind farm, as distinct from a grey seal. Common seals have puppy-like round faces, while grey seals have a straighter, more greyhound-like face, which makes it easy to remember which is which.

Dorothy sometimes swims down to the active part of the harbour, where she seems to derive genuine amusement from playing to little crowds of holidaymakers, splashing about while they wind up their crab lines or wait for the rowing-boat ferry between the Southwold and Walberswick sides of the river. The ferry is a relic from another era. It is just a little wooden rowing boat but has been run by the same family for seven generations and is surprisingly famous among the cognoscenti of such things. The current ferry 'man' is the daughter of the last ferryman and is the author of a book on the history of the ferry, and as all generations of ferrymen have to be, a skilled and strong rower, with an extraordinary knowledge of, and instinct for, the wayward tides and currents of the river. There is a story that elephants crossed the river on the ferry, when it was a chain ferry long ago. There is a faded black-and-white picture of elephants walking along the main street in Halesworth, five miles away. So it could be true.

The River Blyth hides many secrets. Joe Kennedy, the elder brother of J. F. Kennedy, died in a plane crash in the estuary in 1944. Joe Kennedy was taking part in an incredibly brave and dangerous mission, in which Joe and a co-pilot were to fly a Liberator carrying 21,000lbs of explosives, packed into 374 boxes spread about the plane, to a target in France. The Liberator was to become radio-controlled from a point in France and once the radio had locked on, the two pilots were to parachute out of the plane.

The Liberator took off from Suffolk at about 6.30p.m.

on 12th August 1944, but it exploded a few minutes later, with its epicentre over the estuary near Blythburgh, but also scattering burning wreckage along the coast and setting fire to a large area of Dunwich heath and forest. The bodies of Joe Kennedy and his co-pilot were never found. Unwise Americans sometimes come looking for related wartime souvenirs, risking an encounter with the unexploded bombs which still lurk in the Blyth mud flats. Some of the older locals claim to remember J. F. Kennedy visiting Blythburgh, to see the place where his brother died.

If you know where to look, you can see a secret cottage on the banks of the river, on the Walberswick side, quite far up the estuary. It was lived in by a man known as Running Roberts. He used to scare people in Southwold, running about in the churchyard half naked and was considered by many to be half mad, in the days when people used such words to refer to any kind of mental illness or distress. But it turned out that the man was a genius. He was a composer for the Royal Philharmonic Orchestra and he lived on instant coffee and shallow-tinned steak and kidney pies. One night there was a fire at his cottage and 'the authorities' said he could no longer live in his remote riverside cottage but must instead go and live in a nice clean sensible care home. Running Roberts loved his cottage and was desperately sad to leave it. Local folklore says that he just sat silently on the ground with his head in his hands on the night of the fire. But his cottage still houses and hides his piano and his sheets of music and a year's supply of out of date instant coffee and tinned pies. You could walk to Running Roberts's cottage today, right now and see it all, just as he left it, but hardly anyone does, because hardly anyone knows. Teapots still hang in the trees, ingenious self-draining nesting boxes for birds and an indicator of the general intelligence of a man who had a reputation as a lunatic. It is the house that time forgot. But Running Roberts also left a legal legacy on the cottage, that it could never be developed or lived in again. The cottage will remain there as he left it, on the bank of our river, with its piano and its music and its story and its bird-teapots and its instant coffee and tinned pies for eternity, or until the sea comes in to claim it. Future divers and marine archaeologists will be puzzled and perplexed when they find this eccentric domestic arrangement on the bottom of the sea.

Like the Kennedy crash site, the Running Roberts cottage is a secret with a tremendous story, hidden in plain sight. Southwold Harbour and the River Blyth and its estuary are quiet backwaters in a frenzied world, active yet quiet, industrious yet profoundly peaceful, largely man-made yet completely at one with nature. Is it fanciful to see the reflections of mooring and marker posts, squiggled and dappled in the moving water and be reminded of the quieter corners of Venice? It is easy to see other places as more exotic and to miss the everyday beauty right under your nose.

The harbour huts are photogenic, wooden, black and tarred, sometimes on stilts, sometimes ramshackle, but always used by people with a genuine connection with the sea: fishermen, fish huts selling fish straight from their own boats, boat builders, chandlers, skippers and skippers' mates. There are no arty-crafty shops down here, nothing twee. On the Walberswick side of the river there are more tarred huts, including the one for the ferry, along with a few rather more sophisticated timber studios and houses on stilts. To be authentically part of a working harbour, to earn part of one's living from the sea, even if only seasonally and sporadically, is a privilege and an insight.

The jewel in the crown of the harbour is our spiritual home from home, the Harbour Inn, the pub with the 1953 flood level sign above our heads. Here we often sit outside at sundown, watching the sunset, as coastal people do all over the world. Once a year we bring the Household Cavalry Motorbike Tour here. Dogs are not just allowed, but actively encouraged and celebrated. The Harbour Inn has won an award for dog-friendliness. As the sun sets over the river and the marshes, as the afterglow fills our wide skies with vast colour, as geese fly overhead and the eerie cry of a distant curlew breaks the silence, it is possible to feel for a moment an intense sense of contentment, of belonging, of peace. Some may yearn for more glamour or sun, but as we head to the harbour at sundown, we are constantly thankful for this beautiful place. There is no better place than this.

AUGUST

Food in season and local 'sea state' update

Veg
Courgette gluts, pink fir apple potatoes, tomatoes,
yellow and red, all shapes and sizes

Fruit
Greengages and plums

Game
Red deer stag stalking season begins, seasons variable
red/roe stag/buck/doe etc. Muntjac season all year round, sika
and others variable. Grouse from August 12th,
the 'Glorious 12th'

Fish
Dover sole, grey mullet, herring, pilchards, salmon, trout

Beer
Maris Otter barley harvest for Adnams

Distance from cliff
22 metres

Change since last month
No change

Harvest Dust

Summer ends now; now barbarous in beauty the stooks rise
Around; up above, what wind-walks! What lovely behaviour
Of silk sack clouds! Has wilder, wilful-wavier
Meal-drift moulded ever and melted across skies?

Hurrahing in Harvest
Gerard Manley Hopkins (1844-1889)

9

SEPTEMBER

Hunter-gatherers

In the olden days, from Advent in December to Candlemas on February 2nd, rural people exercised a self-imposed celibacy season, to avoid the late stages of pregnancy or care of newborn babies at harvest time approximately nine months later. Our school years still begin in mid-to-late September, to fit in with children helping with the harvest. Our university and academic years follow the same idiosyncratic timetable, even though Cambridge dons seem unlikely wielders of pitchforks in any century. In city, town, village or country, our entire year and calendar is unwittingly organised around 'harvest time'.

The image of the wheat sheaf still adorns suburban toasters and sets of china, a poignant expression of some visceral primitive yearning for a connection with the land and in particular with the harvest, with bread as the central staple symbol. Denby Greenwheat is the mid-century collectors' Antiques Roadshow archetype of the wheat-sheaf-china genre, but there are many lesser versions.

The wheat sheaf also finds its way onto the mismatched tessellated wallpaper patterns typically found in the scruffier student houses. Land girls were central to operations in World War 2. Sting sang a song about walking through fields of barley, 'Fields of Gold', although he shouldn't really encourage his fans to trespass and trample through other people's crops. Neil Young named an album *Harvest*. Martin Parr delights in photographing village vegetable shows, which are essentially a homage to harvest, filtered through his Technicolor eye. The concept of harvest is buried deep in our collective memory and culture, from pagan celebrations via the Bible to contemporary popular culture.

Harvest Festival as we know it was begun in 1843 by the Reverend Hawker of Morwenstow in Cornwall, where he used to sit in what is now called Hawker's Hut, a tiny retreat built into the side of the cliff. Whether the offering is tins of baked beans or elaborate wheat-sheaf-shaped loaves of bread, even the most gritty urban areas still acknowledge harvest.

Large numbers of people migrate across Europe to follow the different harvests, from the cauliflower fields of the Fens to the vineyards of Burgundy, with Suffolk's soft fruit and apple orchards and vineyards in between. But here on our cliff and its surrounding land, harvest time is all about the grain crops, wheat and barley, and the fleets of roaring combines sent to gather them, leaving thousands of acres of glorious golden stubble fields in their wake. The roaring is a magnificent sound, which represents reaping. We are, after all, hunter-gatherers. There is something exciting about spotting the first combine of the year. Or combine *harvesters* as we should correctly call them, for reasons of clarity. The sights and sounds of the combines, as the dust stirs, awakens something deeply embedded in the soul, in the hippocampus seahorse part of the brain, somewhere near the sights and sounds of war-related rituals, the sound of drumming, or the jangling and clip-clopping of a cavalcade of horses approaching, or the susuration sounds of waves breaking over a shingle beach.

There are times when we feel the blood of our ancestors coursing through our veins. Harvest time is one such time. It is a sobering thought that every generation of human beings for the past six thousand years, with the notable exception of the past fifty years, has been and has had to be, directly involved in the bringing in of the harvest to survive.

The place names of villages in the wider territory of the Easternmost House reflect the crops that are or were grown hereabouts: Laxfield, flax field, Linstead, place where linseed is grown, Hempstead, place where hemp is grown, Wheatacre, arable land where wheat is grown, Benacre, arable land where beans are grown, and so on. Many village names end in 'field'. There are times when muck is spread on the stubble fields for miles around, an essential part of the enrichment of the soil and an unwelcome aspect of the bucolic idyll to some of our more sensitive newcomers and second-homers, but I actively like these country smells. Like the smell of earth after rain, they seem healthy and wholesome and clean.

A major change in the visual landscape at harvest time was the introduction of large round straw bales instead of the small rectangular right-sized ones of our childhood. The large round bales are arguably more beautiful in the landscape than the small rectangular bales, but the small bales were portable and held the right amount of hay and straw for domestic-scale animal-husbandry needs. But the real reason we loved the small rectangular straw bales at harvest time as children was that the combination of stubble fields and straw bales created a magical landscape for the ponies. For a few short days or weeks we could ride for miles over vast acres of golden stubble. We could make straw bale jumps approximating to a miniature version of Aintree and pretend to be jump jockeys winning the Grand National. In the golden summers of our childhood, harvest time seemed to last forever.

But the 'golden summers of our childhood' also yielded a spectacle that seems quite incredible in the context of today. In the golden summers of our childhood, the entire landscape would suddenly be ablaze with dangerous stubble burnings. After the harvest, thousands of acres of stubble were routinely set alight. It was completely normal to be surrounded by raging fires and smoke. I remember a Pony Club rally where a giant fireball bounced across the road and onto the grass field where several large groups of us as children on ponies were trotting about in circles or jumping logs. There was a mild sense of drama and the ponies were a bit startled, but the remarkable thing about the fireball incident is that it wasn't entirely out of the ordinary. Inevitably many of these stubble fires became out of control and burnt trees and hedges and unintended fields.

It seems extraordinary now that the stubble burnings were not just allowed but encouraged. Some of the more intensive arable farmers in the 1970s and 1980s also burnt all their straw, as the baling and selling of it was deemed an unprofitable fiddle in the grand scheme of things. From the farmers' point of view, the reasoning behind the burning of stubble was sound. The fires controlled weeds and pests, such as slugs. Whether other animals with a more complex nervous system than the poor slugs were also burnt in the process doesn't bear too much thinking about. Hares live out in the open on exactly the type of arable fields which were burnt. We can only hope they had the instinct to look after themselves, as wild animals so expertly tend to do.

Stubble burning was effectively banned in England in 1993, for pragmatic environmental reasons such as the pollution caused by the smoke and the loss of nutrients in the soil, rather than what might be called social reasons, or anti-social reasons, such as the setting loose of a fireball amid a Pony Club rally full of young children and easily-spooked large animals.

There are some contemporary farmers who would like to bring back the stubble burning and who are lobbying for the ban on burning to be lifted. Their reasoning is that burning stubble controls invasive blackgrass and that as industrial agricultural weedkillers are eyed with increasing suspicion, stubble burning offers a more natural alternative.

The East Anglian stubble burnings were a far cry from the strictly regulated and controlled heather burning on the grouse moors, muirburn, which creates a patchwork of different ages of heather for the grouse and the waders, plovers, curlews and mountain hares who also thrive in that highly managed habitat. Our stubble burnings seemed wild and dangerous and uncontrolled. Yet in my mind's eye, the golden summers of our childhood are filled only with the golden stubble fields of harvest time, with not a fireball in sight. Human memory is a most optimistic editor. Nothing bad ever happens in the past.

The sight of the combines harvesting on the edge of our cliff with the sea in the background is quite spectacular and each year the combine driver has to be wary of how close to the edge he dares to go. Some years, if the erosion has been through a particularly destructive phase during the winter storms, part of the crop has to be left unharvested. The loss to the farm is considerable.

This gentle landscape, which is already quite beautiful when under the plough, becomes even lovelier when the fields around us are all stubble, but of all the many wonders which come with harvest time, one of the most miraculous is the visitation of the geese.

Every year, in September, our clifftop skies are suddenly filled with skeins and skeins of migrating geese. They arrive quite suddenly and feed on the stubble to the north of the Easternmost House, chattering companionably all the time, and they stay for several weeks. The goose is an underrated creature, yet its symbolism is quietly embedded in our culture and folklore. It is the goose who lays the golden egg. In Siena, one of the contradas is the Nobile Contrada dell'Oca, the Noble Contrada of the Goose.

When the geese fly over us in V-formations heading south, it is easy to see how our ancestors believed they carried the souls of the dead. East Anglia was one giant airfield in the war and many pilots would have formed up for brave and fatal sorties from this coast in their Spitfires and Lancaster bombers. Is it fanciful to see the souls of those saviour pilots in our V-formations of geese in flight?

We have much to learn from the geese. Each individual goose is a master of synchronicity. Every goose has to synchronise itself with the entire flock to survive. The goose has to control its body, its movement and its mind, in relation to all the other geese. The goose has to understand the concepts of leadership and followership and fit it with the ever-changing hierarchy of the flock. The goose has to communicate with all the other geese and the goose at the point of the arrow in the V-formation has to decide where to go, and when to relegate itself back into the aerodynamic slipstream of the other geese, to conserve its energy. The geese also seem to have very good social skills, honking gently in flight and chattering among each other when feeding on our stubble.

Although 'our geese' happen to be greylag geese, further up the coast in Norfolk they have pinkfoots and these remarkable qualities seem to apply to all geese. The domestic white goose is a comforting creature, which can live to the age of about twenty-five and is also a good guard dog. Geese are utterly charming and the arrival of our wild geese is one of the great delights of living on our crumbling cliff. I once counted the geese by making a grid and estimating them in tens and then hundreds. There were about nine hundred to a thousand geese on our stubble that day. As with the migrations of other birds like the swallows, one day they will vanish, but we never see them go. We can only wonder where they go and wonder at yet another thousand small miracles of the natural world.

Due to its location and perhaps to some unseen auras from the wind farm, water towers and Sizewell nuclear power station, television reception can be disrupted on our clifftop, just as BBC Radio 4 may suddenly leap across the sea to Dutch radio Zonder Suiker, or some such, during the ironing.

Our favourite clifftop film is Peter Greenaway's *Drowning by Numbers*, which is fortunate since that is the one film we possess. The story takes on a special significance when viewed at the Easternmost House, since most of this pastoral saga was filmed within the extended view as seen from the window: on the beach; around Southwold water tower; along the Blyth Estuary. Which is why we like it. It is very similar to our real life.

We can't see the point of watching a film that would transport us to a totally unrealistic world. It might seem like a waste of time at the end, when we realised that none of it was true. One day, we will have to upgrade the whole of the Easternmost House's entertainment system, but while we wait to make sure our hypothetical new system will not be immediately superseded by something more advanced, we just truck on without much visual entertainment at all, apart from the sea and the washing machine.

Along with Benjamin Britten's *Four Sea Interludes* (*Dawn, Sunday Morning, Moonlight and Storm*), we reckon that with one film and one music CD, we have every single human emotion covered.

As the last of the combines roars along the edge of the cliff, harvesting the Maris Otter barley that goes into the Adnams Brewery visible in the distance, I am once again instantly transported to the golden summers of my childhood: the landscape ablaze with dangerous stubble-burnings; the reassuring weight of a hundred combines rumbling their vibrations through the ground like a distant earthquake; the comforting sounds of farm machinery roaring all through the wee small hours of those balmy summer nights.

The contemporary holidaymakers who have taken to visiting Southwold in recent years seem strangely disturbed by the perpetual racket and harvest dust. But what on earth do they expect in high Suffolk at harvest time? Tranquillity, pastoral picnics, harvest-dust-free air and silence? Not a chance. The roaring represents *reaping*; and the cultural significance of *reaping* is as deeply ingrained into the rural soul as that of hunting.

Crop Circles

As the annual ritual of harvest comes towards its close, thoughts turn to autumnal Harvest Festival rites and all their pagan symbolism, of gratitude and warding-off and of future feast and famine. One such time at the end of summer, we collectively amused ourselves with an artistic agricultural project: creating a crop circle. Someone must have woken up and decided, today we are going to make a crop circle in the blazing sun of what was beginning to be referred to as The Great Drought and, it being a 'close-knit rural community', suddenly there we all were.

It is strange that there have been no crop circles appearing recently. There was a time when they appeared all over the place, overnight. At one stage it was even affecting the harvest yield figures. The aliens, or whoever it was who made them, must have gone through a craze for making crop circles. But crazes, even alien ones, pass. There will always be future crazes, but all are ultimately doomed to end up on the metaphorical compost heap of past clackers, loom bands and fidget spinners. Or in the Design Museum.

But sometimes old crazes are reborn in a wave of nostalgia, as was the case with our one-off retro crop circle revival. Picture the scene, in real time.

The jungle telegraph has rumbled again, rallying the

necessary manpower. The crop circle plan is popular, because we have all been secretly wondering how it is done. The plan is simple. We will make a crop circle, with added appendages, of maximum complexity and accuracy. When it is finished, Roddy and Celeste will fly over it in their little aeroplane to see how accurate it looks and preferably take some photos. After their descent, they will vividly describe the image they have just seen from the air and print out the photos on the hand-held photoprinter they have just acquired. In this way we will be able to judge our crop-circle-making skills and may even discover how the proper ones are made in the process. It will be fun.

One of our number, Mr Holstein-Fresian (not his real name, but he has a dairy herd of that breed of cow and owns the land on which we stand), has planted a Maize Maze on his farm near Southwold, just across the estuary from the 24,000 Blythburgh free-range pigs. The Maize Maze is earning him far more than the whole of the rest of the farm put together. Charabanc-loads of people have been paying to get lost in the Maize Maze, taking little flags with them so that they don't really get lost. They had a few teething troubles with it in the beginning. The maize had grown so much higher and denser than expected, because of the drought, that they really did briefly lose a number of children in the Maize Maze when it opened. The flags solved the problem and if anyone is in there for more than twelve hours, they are rescued by the rescuers on standby. Reggie, who lost an eye in a freak accident with a lucky horseshoe, is one of the rescuers.

He is very versatile in the jobs he undertakes. You have to be, to survive around here.

Planting a Maize Maze is cheating when it comes to agricultural geometry. It is easy to measure and plant such a thing accurately and there are probably instructions on the internet. Crop circles are more of a challenge. Because Mr Holstein-Fresian is making so much money from the Maize Maze, it is his crop that we are going to sacrifice to the crop circle gods. He has kindly lent us one of his hundred-acre wheat fields and has taken charge, because he has an amateur interest in alien-watching and is convinced that we won't be able to do it, which he also hopes to cite as proof of some pet hypothesis he nurtures. The various grain crops are high at this time of year, just getting to their final ripening stage as we reach the tail end of the harvest season. This makes it the ideal time of year for flattening them.

Obviously, it being a crop *circle*, our design is going to have to start with a perfect circle, otherwise we will have failed the task from the outset. The circle will also be a good element from which to judge our accuracy, because we know what a perfect circle is supposed to look like, whereas some of the appendages could be more-or-less anything. We could cheat by saying that the appendages were meant to look like the whatever-it-is they actually turn out looking like. We can't cheat with the circle. With this number of people, it should be quite easy to flatten the perfectly-ripe crop. We are confident of success and most of us are certain that all the crop circles ever made have not been made by aliens, which (assuming we are right about the aliens) proves that it is physically possible.

Our first 'challenge' (or 'problem', in old language) is to get ourselves to the middle of the circle without leaving a messy telltale trail leading from the edge of the soon-to-be-completed circle we are about to make, which would be a dead giveaway of our amateurism in this new arena. We contemplate dropping Celeste out of Roddy's aeroplane as a start. Roddy says that the aeroplane doesn't have a 'hover function' button in it and is therefore not designed to impersonate a Harrier Jump Jet over the centre of the circle. Besides, Celeste doesn't seem to have brought her parachute. It is clearly impossible, so we all trail after each other in single file, until we reach a spot we think might make a good centre-of-a-perfect-crop-circle. As there is some disagreement about this spot, and not everybody stayed entirely in single file, we have already made a bit of a mess of the crop. And we haven't even started properly yet.

Mr Holstein-Fresian is delighted at the mess we have already made of his crop. It strengthens his aliens hypothesis enormously. Some of the more susceptible of the crop circle-makers are wavering in their beliefs. Aliens are the only people who could possibly do it. We have all seen the photographs. Good crop circles are incredibly complicated and extremely accurate, and they *never* have telltale trails from the edge of the field. How else could it be done?

Now that we are in the centre of the circle, we have to

assemble all our string, planks of wood and other potentially useful crop-circle-making equipment and look at the grand plan. Mr Holstein-Fresian has made a wonky little diagram on the inside of a ripped-up packet of Benson & Hedges. He lights a cigarette while we gather round for instructions. Lighting a cigarette in the middle of a one-hundred-acre field of perfectly-ripe wheat at peak harvest time would normally be against the rules. But it is his crop, and the fire brigades are used to crop fires around here. Crop fires are far less frightening than the burning stubbles of our childhoods.

Thank goodness none of the assembled crop-circle-makers has remembered that I am an architect. This is exactly the sort of task architects are good at. I could have drawn the area to scale at 1:100, or even 1:50, based on the Ordnance Survey and with a north point. I could then have planned the whole crop circle, complete with the centre point accurately located from some fixed feature, a radius, 'pi r-squared' and all that and with any oblique appendage-angles clearly marked in degrees. Applied geometry, in other words. The whole thing could have been comprehensively dimensioned in metric (with feet and inches in brackets, because we are in the country here) before we started. I could have probably allocated a team to the circle and another team to each appendage.

I might even have organised a hot air balloon to drop us at the setting-out point at the centre of the circle, to get us started and then take us away, without leaving our amateurish path to the edge. That would be one way of doing it, although I feel convinced that such an architecturally thorough method is not the proper crop-circle-makers' secret, nor is it in the slightly voodoo spirit of the genre. A hot air balloon would be easily spotted and the hot air would be very noisy at night. You'd never get away with pretending to be an alien in a hot air balloon, not even in Suffolk.

We gather round the fag packet plan to see what we are going to create. It looks like one of the stick man drawings illustrating the Old Rectory cricket in the *South Elmham Community News*. No one has a clue what they are supposed to be doing, but we successfully flatten large areas of the crop, using ourselves and our planks. Remarkably quickly, we think we have finished.

It is time for the photographers' over-flight to assess our accuracy. Roddy and Celeste duly take to the air and take their photos. We huddle round the hand-held mini-photo-printer and Roddy presses some of its tiny buttons with the toothpick from my Swiss army Knife, which comes in handy at some point nearly every day. The photos appear. The crop circle looks as if it might have been formed under the helicopter fleet in *Apocalypse Now*. It is certainly visible, but it bears no resemblance to the stick man drawing on the fag packet.

The head, the circle, is an enormous mottled mass of half-flattened wheat, which from a distance looks like a bad case of the mangy fur seen on urban foxes lacking the health-giving benefits of country life. The head has a Teletubby-style wire-coat-hanger appendage, which in turn has what looks like a wiggly piece of string leading out of it. The string is the telltale path of where we entered the field. The stick man body and limbs are really just a few aimless areas of more 'mange'.

The whole thing is a complete disaster. We all conclude that the only way to make a convincing crop circle, complete with appendages, of the complexity and accuracy the crop circle-watching public has come to expect, is to be an alien. Mr Holstein-Fresian is delighted at our ruination of his hundred-acre wheat field. His belief in aliens is confirmed forever.

Post Script

With hindsight, it seems obvious that the photography would have been much easier using a drone, but drone photography for the masses had not really been invented at the time and it is relatively normal round here for people to fly their own tiny private aeroplanes. Also, with hindsight, it might not have been a hundred-acre field of perfectly-ripe wheat that we ruined, but a quiet corner of the farm with a wind-damaged Maris Otter barley crop which had failed some arcane Adnams Brewery quality control test. But the lesson remains clear: crop circles are the work of skilled master-craftspersons worthy of the Worshipful Company of Crop Circle Makers.

SEPTEMBER

Food in season and local 'sea state' update

Veg
Mushroom season starts

Fruit
Blackberry season until 29th, Michaelmas, when the
devil spits on the blackberries

Game
Sept 1st-Feb 1st grey and red-legged partridge;
Sept 1st- Feb 20th wildfowling, duck and goose below
mean high water

Fish
Mussels, oysters, clams, salmon, trout;
Sept 30th generally the end of the wild salmon season,
varies in different places/rivers

Beer
Maris Otter barley harvest for Adnams ends

Distance from cliff
22 metres

Change since last month
No change except two yellow lupin bushes
now on the beach

An East Wind and a Thousand-mile View

Come, worthy Greek! Ulysses, come;
Possess these shores with me!
The winds and seas are troublesome
And here we may be free.

Ulysses and the Siren
Samuel Daniel (1562-1619)

10

OCTOBER

Scale

As an architect, I am used to playing with scale, drawing a building at 1:50, each line one-fiftieth of its real size, drawing a site plan at 1:500, making a model. More usual everyday encounters with altered scale might include reading an Ordnance Survey map or navigating from a road map. Living on a crumbling cliff with a dark night sky and a view of a sea horizon which hints at the curvature of the Earth, encourages consideration of scale on a grand scale, a universal scale, and the effects of thinking about scale in this way can be mesmerising and amusing. To aid consideration of the scale of the universe, imagine you are holding in your hand my small glass globe, a glass marble about two centimetres in diameter, less than one inch across or from its north pole to its south pole, with an equator of pi-r-squared, where the radius is about one centimetre. The main glass globe is made of blue glass and the land masses are mapped out in green glass. One half the globe is almost entirely blue.

Now you have a good idea of the visual appearance scale of this remarkable little glass globe. Imagine now that you have placed a little glass globe in the centre of your kitchen table and then imagine that I too have placed a little glass globe in the centre of the kitchen table at the Easternmost House. Then imagine the distance between your kitchen-table globe and my kitchen-table globe. Then imagine each little glass globe is the size of the actual world, Earth, and you begin to see what a useful thought-provoker this little marble globe can be, scale-wise. If the glass globe is here, on a kitchen table in Suffolk, in England, and is a scale model of Earth, then what in the universe, at the same scale, would be at the equivalent distance away as the tip of South Africa is from Suffolk, or at the tip of South America, or in Tonga? Having begun to stretch the mind in the arena of scale with the help of the marble globe, it is then quite sobering to stand outside on our dark cliff and stare at the night sky. Gradually, as the eye adjusts, the few easily visible stars become many thousands and eventually the Milky Way begins to fill in the dark spaces with celestial clouds of millions of tiny stars, reminiscent of the desert skies of Wadi Rum. What size are all those millions of tiny stars, at the scale of 1:1, actual size? The light left some of those stars many thousands, millions, of years ago, to arrive here our cliff right ... now!

These are the same stars that Julius Caesar saw, or Jesus Christ, or Sir Christopher Wren, who would have understood very well what he was looking at as he was an astronomer as well as an architect. There was a natural crossover in the eighteenth century between mathematics, astronomy and architecture. Thomas Wright, who was an endearing and eccentric eighteenth-century architect, folly builder and landscape designer known as The Wizard of Durham, was also a competent astronomer and was the first person to describe the shape of the Milky Way and to speculate that the clouds of tiny stars were distant galaxies. Thomas Wright was an unsung genius, whose memory is now rather lost to history. He ought to be a national treasure. His life and work would fill a separate book (a book which I have nearly finished writing, as it happens). Like the Easternmost House itself, lost lives and places exist only in the minds of those who know and only if those who know pass on the knowledge to others.

It is impossible to believe that, given infinite time and all the stars and planets in the universe, we are alone. There must be, or have been, some form of life out there. Mars has evidence of water. There are bound to be fossils in the rock, just as there are in our cliff. There must be. It seems too improbable that there isn't and never has been anything alive out there. There are creatures on Earth that can live in the driest desert, that lie dormant, that live in the deep dark sea, creatures we have never even seen. There is no real need to find life on Mars when we have so much fascinating life on Earth. But it would be fun. It would be so exciting to find something, anything, even the tiniest dull life form or fossil which is, or was, alive on another planet. We will. We surely will. Among the many memorable features of Peter Greenaway's *Drowning by Numbers*, not least is that the entire film is a numbers game, is the opening sequence in which a girl is skipping while counting and reciting the names of stars. The names of the stars tend to be Greek or Latin and as a recitation they become a sort of poetic mantra. The skipping-girl aims to count and name one hundred different stars, without tripping over her skipping rope:

1 Antares, 2 Capella, 3 Agropus, 4 Arcturus, 5 Agreeter ... and so on for a further ninety-two names until, with some relief ... 98 Rostra, 99 Procyon, 100 Electra.

The star-counting-and-naming game is at once wondrous, but also oddly boring, which is why there is only a sample tasting menu on this page. It is only the cinematic beauty of the scene in the film, vast shadows of the girl against the whiteness of the house, a house on the cliff in Southwold, which relieves the monotony of her star names. While the idea that there are thousands of stars with romantic Classical names ought to inspire wonder, in fact the opposite effect is true.

By naming and counting them, the stars are somehow reduced, quantified, in much the same way that the sense of awe one feels when standing dead centre under one of the world's great architectural domes is immediately reduced if someone mentions that it took x number of pieces of stone to build it. The attraction inherent in the domes of St. Paul's Cathedral, or the Chiesa della Salute in Venice, or the Mausoleum at Castle Howard, is qualitative not quantitive. Stars and distant galaxies, and the architecture of great domes, are often best enjoyed with a purely instinctive emotional response, just a simple overwhelming unsophisticated sense of wonder, of

Oh!

Wow!

Living on the edge of a cliff all year round means living with all weathers. Sometimes we seem to live on an Italian *agriturismo* farm and other times it is like living on a wind-lashed Falkland Isle. The prevailing weather and winds generally cross from west to east, with occasional warm sirocco winds and occasional cold winds from the north. But the wind that carries the worst reputation is an east wind blowing in off the sea. Rural folklore says that 'When the wind is from the east, it does no good to man or beast', and it is easy to assume that this is a relatively local, at least British and relatively recent, say Victorian, sentiment, but it isn't. If you delve a little deeper into the notoriety of the east wind, you will find that it was the east wind that destroyed the crops in Pharaoh's dream in the story of Joseph in the Bible: 'And behold, seven ears, thin and blasted with the east wind, sprung up after them' (Genesis, Ch 42, v 4). It was also the east wind that brought the plague of locusts. There are several references to the east wind in the Bible and it is almost entirely associated with destruction, which is why the barley grown on our cliff is Maris Otter, a short-stemmed variety with a chance of surviving a battering from the Beast from the East.

The fact that the east wind is associated with destruction in the Bible is an interestingly old example of weather-lore, but it is also revealing, in that as it was written in the Middle East about two thousand years ago, the authors would have had no connection with, or knowledge of, British rural weather-lore, red at night shepherds' delight and so on. While large parts of the Bible are fictional or metaphorical, crop damage from an east wind seems too mundane to invent. They must have been writing from personal experience and agricultural general knowledge, gleaned having observed crops damaged by an east wind with their own eyes. This gives rise to a kind of vertigo of time, in which we have exactly the same experience of crop damage from an east wind as the person or people who wrote Genesis, separated only by two thousand years and two thousand miles. Whatever the faults of the Bible, it is a remarkable repository of human experience and among its more famous and fanciful passages, it also gives excellent practical advice about planting vineyards and curing damp in your house.

October brings the beginning of the winter storms and the accelerated coastal erosion season. Outside, I use ropes salvaged from the beach over the years to lash things down. If ordinary things are left around unlashed in a storm and not shut up in the outbuildings, the force of the wind up here will thrash them all over the cliff. Apart from anything else, a bucket in a hedge or a chair stuck up a tree counts as litter, or a missile.

On a stormy night, sleeping at the Easternmost House is like sleeping in a boat. There is something intensely comforting about being in a relatively cosy clifftop cottage in a violent storm while listening to the Shipping Forecast. Here, the Shipping Forecast is more than an arcane Radio 4 piece of cult Britishness. On our clifftop, it is impossible to listen to the Shipping Forecast without worrying about the large ships at sea, which professional seafarers would refer to as 'vessels' and whose distant lights we may just see on our distant sea horizon. When the Shipping Forecast warns of storms in sea areas North Utsire, South Utsire, Viking, Dogger and Humber, the ships visible from our cliff seem suddenly very tiny and vulnerable against the vastness of the rough seas from the north, their crews in mortal danger. I secretly hope that some combination of fate and nature might hear us when we cry to thee for those in peril, not just on the sea, but by the sea. Specifically, as the storm rages outside, I hope that fate and nature might spare our cliff from excessive coastal erosion damage. But I also know that fate and nature could just flick us away in the wind.

Gumboots

September is the end of summer but only the run-in to autumn proper. October is when real autumn arrives. By October, our cliff's summer sand martins are now safely warm and wintering in Africa, a crop of fat orange pumpkins lie like home-made space hoppers in the fields and all is well. But the gumboots are a bit of a worry.

In the scullery between the larder and the kitchen, there is a long line of gumboots. They are mostly quite large, mostly sludge green or black in colour, some with blue neoprene linings, some with faded labels on the front and buckles on the sides, a few similar blue-blackish ones at intervals along the line and one tiny little red pair of gumboots at the far end. A similar collection of sludge coats hangs above the gumboot line. The curious thing is, I have absolutely no idea who they belong to, or how they got here. Why are there always so many gumboots? Who do they belong to? Where have they come from? Why do all houses in the country (as in country*side*) have similar lines of gumboots and coats, always with some unidentified and unowned, always far outnumbering the head-count of people living or staying in any given house? It is the great rural mystery.

We really should know the answer to these questions. It is worrying, because it can mean only one of two things: either, that there were a large number of people staying with us and we have somehow completely forgotten about them, or, that there are some ghostly gumboot-wearing presences leaving their gumboots in the line.

When people think of us living here by the sea and visit Suffolk only in the summer holidays, they may imagine a perpetual picture book life of deckchairs and beach huts, flags and bunting, picturesque picnics, Walberswick World Crabbing Championships, Thorpeness Regatta, boats, floats and fireworks. They see us cooking fish on a pile of charred driftwood artfully dug into a beach campfire or flying a kite by a sandy dune. Summer visitors to the extended Suffolk coastline seek real-life scenes from *Coast* magazine and *Country Living*. Possibly *Country*

Life. But not *True Ghost Stories* magazine, if such a publication exists. Obviously, we like to make it look easy. We don't want to frighten them and put them off coming to stay. The beach at Easton Bavents is deserted and essentially private all year round, but it is never entirely safe.

The reality, on the cliffs, the beach and the marshes around us, can be rather more brutal, scenes more from *The Field* and *Shooting Times*, P. D. James, brooding dangers, haars, fogs, spooks and sea-frets. As summer finally gives way and the second homes batten down the hatches to lie empty and deserted for the next ten months, locals begin harvesting game from the autumn landscape: pheasants, wild geese, perhaps a pair of mallards with a practised left and right.

Wildfowlers seem to like nothing better than squelching about over mud and marsh, crouching in a dark dyke at dawn or dusk, staring skywards, hoping for a shot at a duck or goose for the pot, happy enough just to be out there, even if they come home empty-handed. The wise go armed with a trust stick and local knowledge, of tides and times, depths and daylight. Even so, the mudflats and creeks can be dangerous and there are tales of knowledgeable men wading through water up to their armpits, narrowly escaping drowning, their total immersion in the moment causing their literal immersion in the landscape, momentarily but lethally having lost all track of time.

'The best time to go lamping for Charlie is on a high tide.'

This is the enigmatic statement of an early-morning

wildfowler down by the river near the marshes, where a month earlier the river would still have been a hot-spot of summer tourism, the same physical place, yet a world away in winter. What he means is that coastal foxes whose range includes the mudflats and foreshore will be driven back onto the marshes by the rising tide and are therefore easier to shoot.

Foxes are predators who have no natural predators themselves, so in the absence of wolves and bears, 'apex predators precipitating trophic cascade', people with vested interests will have foxes in their sights. Predator control to preserve prey species, including game birds, is a fact of rural life. In deep countryside in winter, you will certainly hear the crack of a shotgun or rifle if you live there full-time. But attitudes to predator control are changing, becoming more thoughtful and compassionate, now more likely to be targeting a specific fox to protect specific nests or endangered species, rather than simply reducing overall fox numbers. The RSPB kills foxes (and stoats, weasels, corvids etc.) to save other species, but such organisations talk about their killing and culling in hushed whispers, so as not to upset the public who pay their membership fees. Urban sympathy with saving an individual animal often trumps the conservation and welfare of the species as a whole, when culling is involved in the equation. We need to be able to have a civilised debate about predator control, without getting our heads bitten off. In our nation of animal lovers, such subjects will always be fraught.

Here, in our immediate territory, a vixen shrieks her

calls into the night at the edge of the cliff. A human could track the dog fox in the early morning by scent alone. Although their territory must put them at daily risk from gamekeepers and lamping, 'our' foxes are generally untroubled by rifle or lamp on this farm. There is no need. They freely eat the worms and berries, field voles and wild rabbits around The Warren, without harming anything that would warrant active protection, apart from perhaps a total of five lapwing and curlew nests, at a specific time of year, in a particular area of the farm. There is no immediate vulnerable outdoor farm livestock, apart from our own chickens, which are protected by my chicken-architecture enclosures. Remote-sensing cameras on the outdoor pigs all around us found that fox predation on small piglets was observed, with foxes taking live piglets in the dark just after dusk.

At Somerleyton up the road, the millennial Lord Somerleyton, Hugh Crossley, has introduced a shoot-no-foxes policy on the estate and is genuinely committed to rewilding. It will take a few years to see what the long-term net effect is, on populations of other birds and animals he might want not to be eaten by foxes, but it is indicative of changing attitudes. Contrary to popular caricature, in reality there is a deep rural affection for the fox. As children, when it rained and the sun came out at the same time, we called it a foxes' wedding day. Poor Charlie. It's impossible not to have sympathy with him and his kind, historically a martyr to the ancient rites of wildlife management, just for being a fox.

Anecdotal evidence suggests that the 'disconnect'

between town and country seems to be increasing. This 'disconnect' is evident in casual observations. For instance, if you google 'hay bales' and 'images' many photographs of straw bales come up, captioned as being hay. Every harvest time, there is always a straw-bales-captioned-as-hay-bales photograph somewhere in the public realm. It betrays a fundamental lack of understanding of the difference of hay and straw, what they are and what they are used for, which would have been common knowledge only fifty years ago. The need to save our summer sunshine in bales of dried grass has been essential to our survival in the past and it has also contributed romantically to our language: haytime, haytiming, hay-making, haystack, hayrick, haywire. *Ask the Fellows Who Cut the Hay* by George Ewart Evans (1956) is a classic book about rural life in Blaxhall in Suffolk. 'Jolly boating weather, and a hay harvest breeze...' sets the mood of the *Eton Boating Song*. Straw has none of the historic poetry of haytiming.

Signs of the 'disconnect' are also rife on Twitter, where vegans routinely call dairy and livestock farmers 'harmers'. There are tweets mentioning 'vicious blood-hounds' killing foxes, when bloodhounds have always hunted a human runner, such as the Mitford children, as any fule kno. Giles was the quarry for the Weser Vale Bloodhounds, so we have a fondness for gloomy-faced bloodhounds and their innocent chase. And that's before touching the edges of the widespread confusions between beagles and bugles, trail hunting and hound trailing, harriers as hounds and harriers as birds of prey and so on. Words like 'cowslip' and 'acorn' were famously removed from a children's dictionary, deemed irrelevant in the digital age.

The disconnection between town and country and the loss of knowledge, is not the fault of the disconnected. It is a product of progress and separation from the land. But active hostility, to shepherds and dairy farmers, is the fault of the hostile. For anyone interested to learn, there are many wonderful people with country jobs on Twitter, shepherds and farmers, gamekeepers and stalkers, farriers and thatchers, gardeners and hedge-layers, a huntsman (as in, responsible for care of hounds in kennels, not in the tabloid sense), a van driver who delivers around rural Dorset and countless others, whose main aim seems to be to show people what they do, how and why they do it and how they nurture nature. Used wisely, social media could be a wonderful education tool and a window on other people's way of life and work. Ironically, given its febrile reputation, Twitter could help to bring people together, leaving behind a negative narrative in which 'they' (farmers, landowners, bad) have killed 'our' insects (nature, wildlife, good), so that some crossover of all our Venn diagrams might make it all a bit more 'we', all in it together, all partly responsible, all wanting a nature-rich countryside, schools involved, everyone understanding a little more about the processes surrounding our food and farming.

Perhaps rural words and knowledge don't really matter any more, but the urban equivalent to some of the more factually ignorant and aggressive online campaigns against, say, dairy farming, might be to start a furious campaign to demolish all Palladian architecture, when actually what you meant was to demolish all Brutalist architecture, betraying a startling ignorance of both.

The 'disconnect' is exacerbated by the mainstream media and broadcast media, in which certain kinds of country people are routinely portrayed as rogue yokels or heartless toffs, united by ancient feudal bonds and a shared love of blood, guts, dogs and horses. A rural context also gives tacit permission for use and abuse of the word 'inbred'. For example, in a tweet, a birder relates that he 'had an altercation with some inbred at Easton Bavents', probably having been turned back by the well-known local King Canute, Peter Boggis, for trespassing on a private farm. This farm.

The British character does not like being told what to do, or not to do and if you met any of these supposed rural ruffians as individuals in the pub, or at a cricket match, or in London, when we are not chewing on a blade of grass we are all mingled and muddled up, arch-stereotypes and caricatures among normal-looking people, farmers and fine-art dealers, fishermen and film-makers, retirees and refugees, incomers and IT geeks, all rubbing along together. You would never be able to tell at the outset who did or didn't own a horse, or a gun, or a fishing rod, or a ferret, or go hunting, or shooting, or birdwatching, or live their lives entirely enslaved to a murderous wildlife-killing fluffy cat. Even the most committed hunt saboteurs tend to take off their black-and-camo paramilitary gear and dress as normal people when they are 'off duty'. We have one of the most notorious hunt saboteurs living down the road, who famously desecrated graves in the 1980s, but you'd never know it if you met him out of context.

All the usual clichés of rural stereotypes and caricatures certainly exist, but they have a habit of confounding expectations in unexpected and startling ways, to keep any lazy pigeon-holers on their toes. An elegant 90-year-old former side-saddle hunting thruster is also a concert pianist. An NHS doctor hunts on a cob every Saturday in winter (hounds and the whole entourage following a trail laid in advance by an accountant, in accordance with the Hunting Act 2004). A fisherman gives away the bass he spends hours catching, because he doesn't like eating fish. A vegan skateboard shop owner married a neighbouring organic beef farmer. I could take you to meet them all now.

Back to the ghosts and gumboots, the spirits of the people of our lost villages under the sea are everywhere. Human remains and mammoths are exposed all along the open cliff-face. The ghost of Black Shuck, the local devil dog, frolics joyfully in the waves. The Fishman of Orford is probably still out there somewhere. We are used to ghostly visitations. It is normal here. I just slightly wish that the ephemeral presences had a little beach hut in which to keep their ghostly gumboots and piles of old copies of *Country Life*, instead of leaving them around our house. Unless it is us who leaves things around the house.

As it happens, we may never need the gumboots again. It

has barely rained since the August bank holiday weekend and it may never rain again. You would have thought the extended autumnal sunshine would have made everyone happier, but it hasn't. Farmers are muttering ominously about yields and people in Southwold shops have been referring to The Great Drought for some time, in much the same way as we refer to the 1987 storm as The Great Storm, although the drought isn't really a drought and nor is it great, yet. The vicar who threw so much holy water over Chuffy at the Blessing of Animals service at Blythburgh is worried about it. Creatures from hotter climes have allegedly been sighted and now people are rumoured to be becoming devious about improvised diversion of water supplies.

I thought the whole point of vines is that they like living in a sunny climate and actually require sunshine if they are to produce decent wine, but the hundreds of vines that I planted so laboriously are apparently dying, as a direct result of the drought. Because they were particular varieties from Alsace, *Pinot Noir* and *Pinot Meunier*, specifically chosen to cope with our British rain and to try and make some good quality not-allowed-to-call-it-Champagne, a drought was not what they expected. This is a great shame, considering that almost every other type of vine in the world would surely be able to cope with an English drought. Mr Vine is being very stoical about the vines, but Mrs Vine (not her real name, but she does co-own the vineyards with Mr Vine) is less happy with the drought because of the snakes.

When I have been tending the vineyards during this

so-called drought, hundreds of hours of pruning, tying-in, summer-pruning, de-water-shooting and leaf-thinning to let the sun reach the fruit, not counting the *vendange* which comes in late October here, I have naturally come across many and various creatures. Viticulturally-interested tourists still visit this *terroir* at grape-harvesting and pruning times of year, long after the seaside tourists have gone. I happily answer all their viticultural questions, but they always end up asking personal questions about how I came to be there, surprised and puzzled as to why I should work alone in the vineyards. It seems impossible for many people to understand that I find it physically and financially rewarding to work on the land, when I could be doing something else, like drawing a detail of the allocated dog-bed space in someone's kitchen extension or trying to cram another holiday let into some neglected rustic outbuilding.

Pruning vines is a mesmerising job, requiring concentration and constant small decisions. The same applies to picking grapes, or apples, or any other kind of fruit, although most of Suffolk's orchards have been grubbed up since I was a child. As a teenager I picked apples in the commercial orchards at home for one harvest season, between leaving boarding school and being an au pair. It was hard work, piecework, from 8am to 4pm, half an hour for lunch, sitting on our wood-and-green-canvas hods, chatting, in motley gangs made up of OAPs, French and Dutch students, poachers, pigeon fanciers and public schoolboys. We all rubbed along, all together, all day, with no one at each other's throats. We all knew our apples and we recognised the diamond-pattern planting of the pollinators along the rows, so we never mixed the wrong varieties or sizes erroneously into the bins. It was skilled manual work, not unskilled. It was not all that long ago, but these ordinary British apples would now be considered 'heritage breeds': Egremont Russet, James Grieve, Cox, Discovery, Worcester. And people now seem less inclined to be any kind of pickers.

In the vineyards, I have had an abundance of nature to contend with. Along with all the pheasants and straying muntjac, I have encountered several different types of snake. There have been small green ones which I took to be grass snakes, little bluish silver ones which might have been some kind of worm and a great writhing knot of slimy-looking black ones, the whole writhing knot being about the size of a football. I have even seen a few adders. They all seemed more frightened of me than I of them and slithered gently away into the grass.

It was therefore unfortunate that a snake-o-phobic like Mrs Vine should come across possibly the only really interesting and frightening snake in England, let alone Suffolk, in her own house, no less. Apparently, she was on the telephone in the hall, trying to track down the alpaca-farrier, when a large serpent, allegedly the colour of a liver-chestnut horse, appeared on the stone steps and looked her straight in the eye. It then reared up rather threateningly, just as any domestic cobra might rear, showing the whites of its eyes in the manner of a great, demented, serpentine version of Stubbs's *Whistlejacket*. It then hissed at her, which is, I suppose, what snakes of any kind are wont to do. Interestingly, it was the hissing that frightened her, more than the appearance of a demented, rearing serpent by the telephone. And Mrs Vine is sure the hissing wasn't emitted by a rogue Burco Boiler, the source to which any sudden rural hissing sound can usually be traced.

It was perhaps unwise of me to choose this as the ideal moment to relate to Mrs Vine the story of The Snake and The Baby. The story was told to me by a reliable friend who goes to stay in France at the hottest time of the French summer. Once upon a time, a Provencal baby was snoozing quietly in its pram after lunch, in the cool shade of an olive tree. The Provencal sun was beating down as usual, when a thirsty snake slithered by. Being thirsty, its survival instincts were especially sharp, which is why it could smell the warm milk in the baby's little tummy. The thirsty snake did the sensible thing in the circumstances and slithered up onto the pram, into the baby's mouth and down into its full little tummy to drink the warm milk therein. The protruding tail was espied by a passing olive farmer, or some other suitably romantic character. Many an *ooh la la* and *mon Dieu alors* would have probably been heard at that point and the snake probably slithered gently away into the grass, as they do. But the baby survived.

Picking grapes is a completely absorbing task, up and down the rows, eyes constantly scanning for bunches, quality control re correct stage of ripeness and no mould etc. and the perpetual desire not to miss any good fruit. The birds can have the ones deliberately left for whatever reason, but I hate wasting a crop through my own lack of sharp-eye.

Yet every time I pick a row of anything, apples in the orchards, raspberries and gooseberries in the Old Rec fruit cage, commercial grapes in the vineyards, when I go back down the row to check, I always find I have missed a few. It makes me wonder what 'bunches of grapes' I have missed in my life, hidden in plain sight under a stray leaf.

This is quite separate from the general inquisitiveness about paths not taken and opportunities missed, that if we had done x at x stage of our teens or twenties, we would now be living a completely different life. In my case I nearly married a Californian in my early twenties, so I might now be driving in an open-top car between San Francisco Bay and the Sonoma Valley, never to see an English hedgerow in full May blackthorn blossom bloom again, never to see the great white bursts of cow parsley frothing along the verges of a Suffolk road, never to see a bee orchid or a newly-laid hedge, never to hear the cry of an October pheasant in a tussocky field-edge on a dank autumn evening, never to have need of the words 'peewit' or 'dandelion puff' again.

Knowing that in England it will always rain again soon, proper heavy rain of the kind that drums on tin roofs and runs down the roads in rivulets to water our crops, I suddenly feel grateful that we will definitely be needing the gumboots.

OCTOBER

Food in season and local 'sea state' update

Veg
Fungi, horse mushrooms, oyster, parasol and
field mushrooms, marrows, squashes

Game
Oct 1st – Jan 31st, pheasant, woodcock, mallard,
goose, grouse, hare, muntjac

Fish
March 15th - Oct 6th, wild brown trout season ends

Wine
Vendange at the Suffolk vineyards

Distance from cliff
22 metres, large chunk fallen further along the cliff to the
south

Change since last month
No change, small tree halfway down the cliff

Still Dews of Quietness

Drop Thy still dews of quietness
Till all our strivings cease,
Take from our souls the strain and stress,
And let our ordered lives confess
The beauty of Thy peace,
The beauty of Thy peace.

John Greenleaf Whittier
Hymn/poem, written 1882

11

NOVEMBER

There cannot have been a great deal of difference between living in the eleventh, twelfth or thirteenth centuries. People would have trundled around on their horses and ploughed their fields and scattered and built houses and barns and churches and lived and loved and died and carried on pretty much like that for several hundred more years.

And then one day we woke up and suddenly everyone was zooming around, shaking their impatient fists, hooting at the hapless slowcoaches who only drove at 70 miles an hour and being irritated with people who only checked their electronic devices five times a day, when normal people liked to travel at 100 miles an hour and checked their phones at least seven times an hour, going jabber jabber jabber on keypads all day long, and all night, in a constant approximation of connectedness. What these people, that is, us, failed to notice was that in fact they, we, had become more *disconnected* than any human beings who had ever lived before them: from the land, from animals, from their food, from hunting, from the natural world and most especially, from death itself.

Between these two states, of plodding constancy and neurotic change, came two world wars. The silence at the Cenotaph at 11a.m. on Remembrance Sunday is remarkable because it is now so rare, for anyone, let alone a whole population, to just stop and think. In the past, for generations, we collectively went to church on Sundays, where the initial boredom would have habitually given way to some kind of quiet relief at worst, and an hour's rest and reflection as the norm.

Our ancestors seem to have had an instinctive understanding of the need for silence. Until very recently, people would have gone through their lives with little fragments of solace, quotes learned by heart from poetry or *The Book of Common Prayer,* muddled in their minds, but accessible for comfort at times of celebration or crisis: What is this life if, full of care, we have no time to stand and stare? Drop thy still dews of quietness, till all our strivings cease. Take from our souls the strain and stress. The beauty of thy peace. For our tomorrow, they gave their today. That peace which the world cannot give. Repetition, reassurance, rogation. Dogger, Fisher, German Bight.

The initiation of silence is itself a form of saying something.

The beginning of November is characterised by allusions to death. Bonfires and the burning of effigies, the eleventh hour of the eleventh day of the eleventh month,

Remembrance Sunday. Ranks of ancient men with memories and medals. The hunting season begins, with opening
meets of hunts throughout the land. The shooting season
is in full swing. The news reports an ageing population
about to die of cold. The Suffolk Punch, our uniquely
Suffolk horse (always chesnut without the 't'), is on the
brink of extinction. Starve Gut Corner reminds me what
happened if a farm girl accidentally found herself 'in
the family way', in the days of yore. No life seems safe.
War is said to be 99% boredom and 1% sheer terror and
our clifftop weather at this time of year reflects the grim
theme. Days of silent gloom are punctuated by violent
cracks of storms and cliff-falls. People affected by loss
of daylight sink into their seasonal depression, a kind
of mental-health hibernation. The dreaded Christmas
word begins to loom on the horizon, which exacerbates
the misery for many. And at the edge of England, all of
nature seems in accord.

'Remembrancetide' nudges half-remembered phrases
learnt from Wilfred Owen to stir from their peaceful
graveyards in some quiet corner of the brain, adding to
the intangible sense of imminent grief. The old lie, *dulce
et decorum est pro patria mori*, anthem for doomed
youth, what passing bells for those who die as cattle? The
doomed youth seems to include the young of our native
wildlife, the adolescent fox, the teenage vixen, the lithe
leveret, although all are far from 'defenceless' and nor
are they 'innocent', blessed as they are with nature's gifts
of guile, speed and amoral instinct. Ribbons and flowers
are tied to trees at the sites of young lives lost, driving

too fast in the dark. Even the marauding muntjac seems uneasy, as if prey to some premonition of death.

Much of this is in our collective memory rather than in the present day, but 'race memory' is long and can take many centuries to exorcise. Just when the tension becomes unbearable, some minor public figure sparks the annual row about the rights and wrongs of wearing poppies, too early, not before November, poppy fascism, virtue signalling and the right of so-and-so not to wear a poppy on television. And then we know we are soon to be saved. The tension finally lifts at precisely eleven o'clock at the Cenotaph.

Nimrod and *Dido's Lament*. The Union Flag. God, Queen, Country. Not at the Remembrance Day service at the Cenotaph, but at the funeral of Mrs Boggis in Southwold church, the local matriarch since 1953, a Suffolk farmer's wife given the rural equivalent of Churchill's state funeral. *Nimrod*, *Dido's Lament* and the Union Flag were augmented by the *English Hymnal*'s Greatest Hits: *Jerusalem, I Vow to Thee My Country,* the lot. The back of the service sheet had a picture of her black Labrador sitting under her shredded Union Jack (as we are now allowed to call it, by the official flag-etiquette aficionados who decide these things) which Mrs B flew from a flagpole outside her house in all weathers, all year round. Had she lived to see the EU referendum, I suspect she might have voted for Brexit.

Certainly, Mrs B was the caricature of a Brexit stereotype, and yet, living and working in the British countryside, surrounded by apparent stereotypes whose opinions run counter to all prejudiced expectations, I also know that she might actually have voted Remain. Her five children were of young-parenting age, so she was well-connected generationally and at her great age, she was worldly. Assumptions of 'You lot think x' are often confounded by real life. Most reasonable people have a well-developed 'radar for nuance'. From the vantage point of the future, we can look back on every century and see that there was mostly positive progress.

As the massed bands of the Household Division strike up *Nimrod* at the Cenotaph and the man with the cymbals crashes his great dustbin lids together at oddly unpredictable moments to emphasise the point, we fall into a rare act of national togetherness. The weather is set at 'crisp, autumnal sunshine', which seems appropriate for the diminishing ranks of bright OAPs who served in the last old-school war that affected everybody in the country. Villages gather round war memorials across the land. And then comes the Silence, and the thoughts.

I think of my mother's father and of the painting of him on a horse, with a pack of hounds at his feet, a large and solid country house symbolically in the background. Everything in the scene was destroyed by the Second World War. The man was killed. The house was requisitioned and eventually demolished. Yet I recently stood in the very same place and the setting and atmosphere was still recognisably the same as I remember it as a child. I think of how Granny told us she lied about the horses and hid them from the army requisition scouts and how she used to drink the vegetable-water for the vitamins. I think of

Mr Keefy, the Irish wolfhound who was put down during the war because it was deemed immoral to feed him so much meat, when even with wild rabbits and pheasants, people needed the food. I think of the 'doubly-thankful' village of St. Michael South Elmham, not far from our clifftop. The Lancashire Pals. That grainy black-and-white footage of young men jauntily waving and smiling at the camera, thinking they were on their way to great adventure. The haunting eyes in that photograph of a man carrying his friend on his back in the trenches. Millions of names, carved in stone with pride. Every letter and serif, with extra care. Eton and Winchester war cloisters. Trinity College, Cambridge. The Unknown Warrior. All equal in death. And I think of Wilfred Owen, his peerless words, and his mother, who learnt of his death on the morning of the day the Armistice was declared. And I want to weep. Even thinking about it now I want to weep. But the old-school training kicks in and the stiff upper lip remains strong. And at last, the trumpet sounds reveille, and the Silence is over for another year.

I believe humour to be a vital survival mechanism, which may explain why certain people are prone to getting the giggles at the most inappropriate moments. In church, at a funeral, someone in the pew exactly behind you will sing *I Vow to Thee My Country* so startlingly badly, ranging up and down the musical scales as if climbing Mount Everest, in random sonic bounds so sharp, flat, discordant and just plain crazy, that it is impossible not to feel the errant giggle rise. You stare at the service sheet, even though long years of childhood training mean that of course you know all the words off by heart already. At a wedding, during a fire-and-brimstone sermon, you think that if you just keep on breathing and thinking of nothing and don't catch the eye of anyone, this too will end and all will melt away, yet the torture continues. What was nature thinking, giving some of us this ridiculous defence against terror and danger? The method that works every time, to quell unbidden mirth when it arises, is to revisit that deep Silence at the Cenotaph, and the thoughts that go with it.

There are times when during a thunderstorm, with waves crashing against the cliff and making the house shake, I suddenly find the whole situation overwhelmingly amusing. Us tiny pointless imps, sitting on a tiny pointless dot in the infinity of space and time, the indifferent universe not giving a damn, and yet our cares and cultural treasures seem so important. And they are. The Cenotaph is sacred. For now. But living on the edge of an eroding cliff at the mercy of nature gives a different perspective on time and human influence. You start to take the 'Trinity College, Cambridge, four-hundred-year cycle long-term view', and wonder what England will be like in two hundred, three hundred, four hundred years' time. Will people still gather at the Cenotaph? Will the memory of our wars gradually recede into the mists of time and mythology, like Agincourt? How will rising sea levels and climate change affect the landscape, the trees, the plants, the birds, the animals, the crops, the people, nature itself?

There is from time to time a State of Nature Report,

which is worrying in its affirmation that our wildlife is dying out, that numbers of even the most common animals and birds, like rabbits and sparrows, are down. We are on the edge of a mass extinction, an 'ecological apocalypse'. And it's our fault. The pressure of human activity and in particular post-war agriculture, on nature is causing irreparable damage. We must ban agrochemicals, have fewer children, eat only plants, stop travelling, plant trees, boycott palm oil, drink almond milk imported from California. Oh, hang on, that last one surely can't be right. It all seems too doomsday, exaggerated by the voices of people whose 'brand' is to make a living out of writing and talking about environmental controversy, and who therefore counter-intuitively have a vested interest in ecological bad news, just as a dentist has a vested interest in people having damaged teeth, since healthy teeth would put him out of a job.

Having known our Suffolk farming 'wildlife desert monoculture' landscape all my life, I feel more optimistic. On this farm alone, there are wild areas, scrub areas, acres of habitat land, hedges, wildflowers and gorse, all alongside the main crop, Maris Otter barley for Adnams beer. Hedges ripped out when I was a child have been replaced. Field margins are left long. Attitudes to 'vermin' have completely changed in one generation. Old woodland is nurtured and new woodland has been planted. Farming is gentler. Gardening is wilder. People are kinder. Rivers are being re-wiggled. We are once again cherishing life. The tide has turned.

NOVEMBER

Food in season and local 'sea state' update

Veg
Parsnips, red cabbage, celeriac

Fruit
Apples, quinces, medlars

Nuts
Chestnuts, hazelnuts, walnuts

Game
Pheasant, partridge, mallard, grouse, hare, rabbit, muntjac

Distance from cliff
19 metres, measured loss is more than it appears visually

Change since last month
Big loss of 3 metres, psychological change,
now less than 20 metres left

Ring of Bright Water

To everything there is a season,
and a time to every purpose under the heaven:
a time to be born, and a time to die;
a time to plant, and a time to pluck up that which is planted;
a time to kill, and a time to heal;
a time to break down, and a time to build up ...

Ecclesiastes, Ch 3, verses 1-4

12

DECEMBER

The White Hart

December brings out the pagan in all of us, masquerading as something other than paganism. We find ourselves sucked into ancient traditions, gathering armfuls of holly and ivy from the hedges, harvesting mistletoe from upper branches in overgrown orchards, bringing fir trees into the house, laying fires and lighting candles, bringing light to the time of greatest darkness, and contemplating the unseasonally odd timing of a newborn baby in a manger in a stable, when normally nature decrees that baby animals are born in spring. The imagery of a British winter is still bound up with nostalgic tropes of snow and robins, fir trees and cottages, olde worlde scenes of horses and hounds and visions of London involving lamplighters and pubs, coaches and horses, and the Household Cavalry clip-clopping along in 'cloak order'. Stoats, mountain hares and ptarmigan (white grouse) are miraculously transformed in white ermine, fur and feather, nature's camouflage against the snowy uplands.

Here on our windblown cliff we do not have any snowy uplands or deep drifts, but we do have white animals and in particular white deer. There is more than one 'white hart' nearby, because I have seen one with antlers and one without. The 'white hart' with antlers I saw further down the coast on the heathery heathland. It had the conformation of a young red deer stag but was entirely white. Talking to a professional stalker, an expert paid to selectively thin the herd for its own long-term benefit, I gleaned that red deer can occasionally be albino, to become 'white red deer'. There is one such young albino stag living in the woods near Dunwich Heath, well-known to the few local stalkers, but mostly unseen and unknown by the public at large. My sighting of it at dusk, on the way from A to B and vaguely looking out for a small herd of Exmoor ponies who are employed for 'conservation grazing' duties, was entirely down to luck. I didn't see the Exmoor ponies, but I did see the prehistoric-looking Konik ponies who do the same job. And I also chanced to see the white stag.

White deer, who would historically have been more vulnerable to predators, tend to be spared by stalkers for romantic and heraldic reasons, and so they now have a paradoxical Darwinian advantage, much as on most shoots there is a fine for shooting a white pheasant.

Nearer to home, on the edge of the woods at our end of 'our' beach, where the Benacre estate begins, I have several times seen a 'white hart' with no antlers. From its size and shape, this is likely to be a roe deer, which can be naturally white without the mutation of being albino. The woods are full of pheasants and the estate is 'keepered', meaning the gamekeeper will be keeping a watchful eye on predators, including greyhounds and other rural rogue cur dogs exercising their 'right to roam' when they dint orta (Suffolk for shouldn't). Gamekeepers and shepherds may shoot dogs which chase their charges. As we no longer have any wolves or bears in these woods, our local 'white hart' not only survives but thrives.

Through trial and error, and silent stalking taking account of the wind direction, as one might be taught by a ghillie at Balmoral, I have worked out that I am most likely to see the white deer grazing on the near edge of the wood where there is a glade bounded by woodland, reedbeds and beach. It is a private, sheltered spot that must feel relatively safe to a prey animal whose flight instincts remain sharp and who cannot know that there are no 'apex predators' waiting to pounce on it, nor that the human predator tends to spare the white deer. White deer probably cannot even know that they are white.

On one such white-deer-stalking and wood-collecting venture (a rural walk always needing some kind of greater purpose), I happened upon some men with ropes and assorted 4x4s of the 'country-cred' variety, farm pick-ups, that sort of thing. Slightly alarmed that I had disturbed some dark arts of poaching or pillage, and therefore might need silencing and dumping in the reedbeds, I planned that when I reached them I would do what country people generally do and greet them with a cheery 'hello' or 'good evening', perhaps with a slight wave, while striding purposefully onwards so as to avoid being easy to catch and dump in the reedbeds.

In this frame of mind and at that time of nearly-nightfall, I was therefore slightly surprised when these 'entrepreneurs' hailed me as friend not foe. As I approached, on further inspection, these entrepreneurs were indeed 'friends', of the loose-rural-connection type who had perhaps played for the farmers at the Old Rec cricket or similar, and they had cooked up a plan to make money from a natural resource on the beach: stumps.

In HRH the Prince of Wales's garden at Highgrove, there is a woodland feature known as the 'stumpery', in which various impressive tree roots and stumps have been artfully arranged to be a visually interesting punctuation point to garden-wanderers, as well as an ideal habitat for mosses, insects and small creatures of the woods. 'Someone' had noticed that there are some huge tree roots and stumps artfully arranged all over our beach, with the added advantage of being weathered and bleached, some to a white bone-like quality, some apparently fossilised and others deeply ingrained with swirling lines. Just the sort of thing one might want in a Highgrove-type garden stumpery.

These local entrepreneurs, who shall remain nameless, had somehow identified a visitor down from London in the summer holidays, who had expressed a desire to out-stump the stumpery at Highgrove at her house in the country, in a shire somewhere to the west of London. The house in the country is apparently her third 'home', after the one in Southwold and the one in London. All this information is a clue that the entrepreneurs may include coastal as well as farming folk, since farmers seldom have much contact with visitors from London, except perhaps to offer them farm diversification recreations or holiday-let accommodation. The subject of the roots and stumps on the beach had been discussed in high summer and then forgotten. Until now. Conveniently, it was on a remote part of the beach in mid-winter, at a dark-ish time of day, that the enterprise had once again been encouraged back to life.

Using all the most appropriate clawing and lifting equipment that one might find on, say, a farm or a working harbour, the artful roots and stumps were man-handled into position to begin their new career, disrupting their many years of fossilising in the Suffolk sun, and I might add, removing some of the more interesting and attractive features of 'our' garden, the beach. It begged several questions, one of which is, if some beautiful old tree roots are strewn around a beach, to whom do they rightfully belong? The legal answer is, it probably depends on things like private ownership of the foreshore and high and low tide lines. The emotional answer is, not you! And certainly not someone from seven counties away who wants to out-stump the stumpery at Highgrove.

In fairness to the rural entrepreneurs, the price was £3,000 per root or stump, allegedly, and the beach is still strewn with artful roots and stumps too big to move, so nature as always had the upper hand and the last laugh. I did see the white hart on that particular sortie, but I kept it a secret from the entrepreneurs, just in case their extravagant stumpery-fancier might turn their attention to deer-taxidermy and seek to out-Balmoral Balmoral.

Ring of Bright Water

I sit in a tarred-timber hut, with a brindle sea-leopard of a greyhound asleep before the stove, which crackles and spits from the salty timber scraps burning within. Rough beach-foraged wood is stacked beneath, in a salvaged ring of blackened steel whose metal plate protects the boarded floor. Beyond the door is the river, the sea a stone's throw distant, and encircling, mist-hung reedbeds. A little group of terns sweeps past the window. But for the fire and the background breathing of the sea, there is utter silence.

If you think I have plagiarised the opening paragraph of *Ring of Bright Water*, you are right, but it is for two reasons: to end with a beginning, and to bring to your mind a circle. Gavin Maxwell wrote other, better books, but the idea of a ring of bright water captures the theme of continuum in a beautiful and evocative image, and it is entirely congruous here, since our territory is enclosed by our own ring of bright water: a ring of reedbeds, river and sea.

There is comfort in the cyclical certainty that spring will return after these, the shortest darkest days and that summer suns will return to warm the earth. The simple fact the sun will always rise tomorrow has so become mired in religiosity and astrophysics that the balm of its elemental truth has been lost. Wilfred Owen's poem

'Futility' is essentially about the sun, and seems to be a tremendous affirmation of life, not really about the futility of war and death at all: *'If anything might rouse him now/ The kind old sun will know./ Think how it wakes the seeds,/ Woke, once, the clays of a cold star.'*

All we need to know is that the sun will always rise tomorrow and on our cliff we will be the first to see it. The truth is, everyone has a cliff coming towards them, the difference is we can see ours. Our moment of life is brief. Usually the erosion is gradual and predictable. Occasionally, there is an unexpected sudden cliff collapse. An RNLI sign on the side of the Lifeboat Station down at the harbour warns that '8 dogs', crossed out, '9 dogs' have recently fallen into the river. The advice is to put your dog on a lead near the harbour wall and be aware of the tide tables. But then something else will happen. A man was killed by a cliff collapse a few miles to the south. Gentle-looking dangerous places like this bring to the fore the intriguing aphorism, *'Man anticipates all, save that which befalls him.'*

The idyllic vision of the private Avalon exists primarily in the imagination, as a place of succour and pilgrimage, to be visited vicariously, and often enjoyed most intensely by people who could not begin to live with no running water in a remote Highland location, for example, nor on a windblown clifftop, for that matter. However, it has come to my notice that when these places do exist in real life, it seems to be an essential ingredient of their mystique that they must end up being physically and violently destroyed.

Henry Beston's timber shack, the little house of *The Outermost House* on the headland at Cape Cod, was swept off its foundations by a massive winter storm. The house at Sandaig, the centre-piece of the Camusfearna of *Ring of Bright Water*, was completely gutted one night by a frightening fire, and later, coincidentally, its remains were bulldozed to the ground just before Gavin Maxwell's remains were interred at the spot where it had stood, as if the house itself could not exist except within the fable of his life.

Our beloved little cottage, the Easternmost House, which by now I hope feels as real and familiar to you as it is to us, carries with it this ethereal quality too, and must perish. I imagine that one day, before we are ready to go, the cottage will be carefully unbuilt, its materials salvaged but its soul removed. The cheerful demolition crew will smash through the windows which have framed our private sunrises and moonlit seascapes. The yellow digger will destroy the walls where our familiar pictures and photos hang. Then the sea will finally come, and it will devour without gratitude the ancient piece of cliff upon which the house now sits. And afterwards, this spot where we have known a happiness beyond contentment, will remain and exist only as thin air and seabed.

The summer suns and the cold salt-winds will not notice its absence, nor ours. Wherever else we may be called away to, by circumstance or the desire for adventure, this little territory will remain our spiritual home, our private Avalon of light and water and sky. The sound of the oystercatcher on a June evening when the days are longest will stay with me forever. This place has quietly taught us how to carry its still small voice of calm within us, always and wherever we go. Yet while there is time there is the certainty of return. There is no better place than this.

Conclusions and Future

Living with erosion has changed my perspective on life. I have become more tolerant of wild nature, more fatalistic and *laissez faire*, or *laissez vivre*, about wild plants and animals that in the recent past and by our collective conventions would have routinely been attacked by one of the four horsemen: poison, mower, strimmer or gun. Even ragwort, one of the earliest plants I learnt to recognise as a child (after nettles and dock), as a poisonous enemy that could kill ponies, has its place up here on the edge, far from the nearest horse, a home to caterpillars which will become butterflies. On our cliff, we have gone a bit feral.

The lapwings and curlews who nest on the farm are left largely undisturbed, their exact locations a secret, except to say that they have fledged successfully in an area close to the edge of the cliff. In other parts of the farm, there is an abundance of prey, field voles in the rough edges, rabbits in The Warren, and rural rats and mice around the ruined farm buildings. The combination of easy prey and location seems to protect these endangered birds from predation by foxes, but also to be factored in is that most of the land around here is either 'keepered' for shooting, or farming neighbours go out lamping at night, so the numbers of foxes are monitored closely, just not by me. The slight mystery is why lapwings and curlews are not predated more often by birds of prey, but that too might be because there is so much other and much easier prey available: rabbits, voles and mice out and about, and probably less careful and less well camouflaged when seen from above, than the remarkably invisible nests hiding their speckledy eggs and chicks. One of the most endearingly comical characteristics of wader chicks is that their tiny fluffy bodies have yet to grow into their enormous wader feet.

I genuinely believe carefully planned territory-marking by male dogs to be an under-used natural method of predator deterrent. I walk Chuffy on his lead, in deliberate arcs described as if drawn on a plan, to form a nest-area boundary. When we go on dog patrol, Chuffy marks this territory to warn off the foxes as clearly as if I had buried an electric fence. The day after Speedy died, a fox killed our then three very tame pet chickens in broad daylight. Speedy was a large male greyhound, 'uncut' and 'entire' (as in, alpha and male, to a fox), and he had protected these chickens for seven years of free-range life, during which not one chicken was killed, out scratching about all day and only shut up at night. Invisible scent boundaries are a genuine asset to ground-nesting birds, according to my unscientific research.

The *laissez vivre* policy extends to moles and rats. I have always rather liked moles, in literature and in real life, from Moldy Warp the Mole in the *Little Grey*

Rabbit books to Mole in *The Wind in the Willows*, and my admiration for the brown rat has increased immeasurably through observation. Rats are adaptable and resourceful creatures, climbing trees and walls to steal food intended for the birds, yet hardly ever seen, minding their own business and living discreetly somewhere under the various farm buildings. Our rural ratties are really no bother. Ratty in *The Wind in the Willows* was actually a water vole, but there's not much difference zoologically, between a ratty and Ratty, yet one is reviled and the other cherished.

'Better in early youth and strength the race for life to run/ Than poisoned like the noxious rat or slain by felon gun,' says the old fox in *The Fox's Prophecy* (by D. W. Nash, 1870), a fascinatingly prescient poem of 75 stanzas, and well worth googling, which also includes the line, 'For swiftly o'er the level shore/ The waves of progress ride; The ancient landmarks one by one/ Shall sink beneath the tide'. In context, Nash seems to mean metaphorical as well as literal landmarks will sink beneath the tide of progress. 'Noxious rat'-wise, I have never needed to call in the Sealyham terriers for a morning's ratting, although in theory I would and I disapprove of poison because of the cruelty, and the barn owls.

While coastal erosion draws attention to the physical erosion of the landscape, there are invisible threats which could erode the countryside as surely as the North Sea eats away at this farm. The threats to rural life as it currently exists are many and variable, including a tsunami of hostility enabled by social media, but when combined, they could cause great change to both the functioning of the countryside and its physical appearance. In no particular order, these invisible threats include, but are not limited to: opposition to sheep, sheep farming and sheep farmers; opposition to livestock and dairy farming; opposition to lawful forms of hunting, shooting and fishing; opposition to grouse moors; opposition to private land ownership; opposition to many aspects of the horse world, especially National Hunt (jump) racing and the Pony Club and more glibly, opposition to and antipathy towards tweed and the wearers of tweed. This is not an exaggeration. It is increasingly real and vehement. This combination of rapidly changing attitudes plus social media is the metaphorical 'North Sea' to which the countryside must adapt.

I would like to see the living, working British landscape thriving as it has for generations, while acknowledging the need to evolve and adapt, at least in some places, to the needs and values of a now predominantly urban population. There is a place for rewilding, as part of a mosaic or patchwork of different habitats and land uses, and it is an intriguing concept, but for rewilding to be effective at landscape scale, it must work alongside and in collaboration with existing local people, farmers, shepherds, gamekeepers etc. respecting and employing their skills and knowledge. What rewilding seems to mean in its currently ill-defined form is the imposition of an unproven experimental grand plan, by outsiders with a niche interest but with no demonstrable rural skills, to the exclusion of the working landscape, its history, culture and people. The few working examples of re-wilding we have in Britain, so far, tend to be on inherited traditional estates, including farming and shooting, or on large areas of the Highlands, more recently bought by the very rich, for pleasure, but with no real need for economic viability.

Knepp Castle is a house with an estate which includes an arable farm now converted to a kind of organic farm-animal safari, a Sussex Serengeti, and is perhaps the nearest example we have as a working model of rewilding in practice, or more accurately, wilding. But it still involves the breeding and killing of grazing animals for meat, so as a model it is directly at odds with the vegan lifestyle proposed by some of the most prominent proponents of rewilding. There is a gap in the market for a financially viable working example of true rewilding, crowdfunded by supporters of the theory of it, and complete with vegan ethos, to show the existing upland farmers and grouse-moor owners how to do it, as a 'not like that, like this' demonstration of the benefits to nature and people.

Knepp Castle shows an attractive version of one possible future of farming, with longhorn cattle grazing alongside Tamworth pigs and wild deer in what looks like ancient prehistoric woodland, but Knepp is in Sussex, an accessible home county, near motorways, and was inherited from grandparents not parents (meaning initial criticism of unconventional farming methods was only from farming neighbours, not more awkwardly from knowledgeable farming parents who had devoted a lifetime to the estate), so had some very particular conditions in its favour from the outset.

Perhaps we need to put natural history on the national curriculum, including wildlife management and death, killing and culling. 'Town' or 'country' is a state of mind, not distinctly related to living here or there. The chasm between opposing ways of life must be bridged. We have to rub along together, town and country, dog person and cat person, vegan and omnivore, shepherd and #sheepwrecked, ecotourism and shooting, pro and anti, left and right, over and under, side by side.

The physical destruction of the land from coastal erosion is the most visible threat to the countryside, but the cultural erosion may turn out to be more damaging in the long term.

Traditional country life must evolve and adapt if it is to survive in the modern world of hyper-connectivity, a camera in every pocket. Mysterious rural practices like gamekeeping and deerstalking could be openly explained. Hunting with hounds could continue, but with packs of hounds following a trail of some standard identifiable scent, like Dettol, which would be anathema to the true hound-work purist but might be a realistic way of continuing hunting activity, culture and tradition into the future, saving hounds and hound shows, kennels and puppy shows, and preserving some connection with the art of venery. Shooting could continue, but with smaller bags, fewer birds shot, more walked-up days instead of driven and every single bird cherished as food. If any bird is not going to be eaten, it must not be shot. Live and let live. Compromise. Good manners and tolerance on all sides. A typically British muddle.

There is scientific research on erosion, and Churchillian talk about resilience and fighting on the beaches, much of it seemingly pointless. Nothing can stop the almighty power of nature and the wise money might be better spent on thinking about how best to adapt to the erosion, how to accommodate it and how to accept it. It is a bit like accepting that with a late cancer diagnosis, treatment is probably, factually, futile. Over a single night, we have seen a whole dune disappear, or the whole coastline of two counties be covered in sawn timber from a single ship. People come and measure the cliffs, from the top, from the bottom, on the beach, from the air, with lasers, with drones and with clipboards. But none of this measuring changes the reality on the ground.

The east coast is a soft landscape, not easy to defend even if the money was available. I have researched what people do in other countries and there are some clever ideas to hold back the sea. Some suggest sand bags impregnated with the seeds of tussocky grasses, so that the grasses bind the sand bags together to form a soft sea defence. Others claim that if the cliff can be stabilised at 42 degrees, it will remain stable at that angle and not be eroded. But I can't believe any of these people have lived with or observed the true power of erosion for any length of time. It all seems too theoretical, too computer-modelled, too Pythagorean.

The sea moves ancient forests and old wartime concrete tank-traps overnight. It dumps whole beaches of shingle in one tide. Then it takes it all away again. Sand bags smaller than a house would be flung about by the waves with disdain. The dune slope was almost precisely at the magic 42 degrees the day before the entire dune was engulfed by a single tidal surge. In other languages the word for flooding is 'inundation', and the tidal surge was exactly that. Here, even if it was feasible, building soft sea defences all along the cliff would cost a fortune, just to save some sandy farmland, gorse-scrub, a scruffy cottage and the ruins of a few old farm buildings. The waterfowl, larks and lapwings will live in peace without us, and the sea will roll in over the land.

The birds and animals will adapt to this natural phenomenon, a vastly greater and more authentic example of rewilding than a half-tame fenced-in pack of Highland wolves would be. Besides, not only is it illegal to fence predators in with prey animals, even if the enclosure is a 20,000-acre estate, but well-intentioned rewilders and landowners who advocate deliberately controlling wild deer numbers with privately-owned, human-introduced packs of wolves may find themselves prosecuted under the Hunting Act 2004, depending on the precise legal definition of a 'dog'. *Canis lupus*, the grey wolf, is taxonomically a 'canine', so any person intentionally acquiring and releasing wolves to hunt deer would seem to come under 'Hunting with Dogs' in the eyes of the law. Wolf kills are also messy, so the issue of unnecessary cruelty to deer must also arise, regardless of the legal status of hunting with wolves, or it being considered 'natural'. Co-existing with and managing wildlife in our enlightened age is a moral minefield.

Tracer pebbles are used to measure the drift of shingle along the coast. Normal pebbles are drilled with a hole and glass tags containing information like that of a bar code are inserted and sealed in. Then the tracer pebbles are put back on the beach and monitored, much in the same way as birders tag birds to follow their movements. Some of the information (about the birds or the pebbles) may be helpful, but much of it seems misleading, not telling the whole story, or just dull. Bland data in search of a storyline.

I have found that living with coastal erosion offers a wider perspective on the world, and an outlook much along the lines of Stoicism, a Hellenistic philosophy founded in Athens in the third century BC that feels oddly contemporary. Life is short. Live in the moment. Our moment of life is brief. The world is unpredictable, but we can control ourselves. Practise for misfortune. Rehearse worst-case scenarios. Choose not to feel harmed and you won't feel harmed. Meditate on your own mortality. Keep a journal. Remember how small you are. Everything is ephemeral. Take the view from above. Don't try and control things that are out of your control.

Stoicism in popular usage conjures images of bleak boarding schools, boys with stiff upper lips having cold baths every morning and never crying, before embarking on a lifetime of emotional repression, missing Nanny and being physiologically unable to say 'I love you' to their wives or children. But that cliché is a Spartan image, and seems unfair to the original Stoics, whose ancient philosophy is supremely practical and applicable to modern life. To practise negative visualisation, for example, is sound advice. Imagining and rehearsing the deaths of the people (and animals) close to you, can be helpful in coping with these events when they actually happen. Stoics prepare themselves.

Take the view from above. This exercise in Stoicism is simple but clever. If you literally imagine looking down on the world from above, from a great height, so that you can see all the people, all the families, the farms, the feuds, the weddings and divorces, the births and the deaths, everything becomes more manageable. More normal. A shared experience. Everything that happens to us has almost certainly happened to someone else. We are tiny.

Our cliff is in crumbling country, at the edge of *a* crumbling country. Long-term maps of rising sea levels show the predicted future shape of Britain, with most of Norfolk and Suffolk under the sea. The Wash will spread over several counties. Coastal erosion will continue, past the hundred-year line, past the two-hundred-year line. But eventually, the erosion of the crumbling country will come up against the hard country, the stone, the Pennines, the Welsh mountains and castles, the Fells, the Highlands, Applecross, Arkle and Foinaven (Foinavon being the Grand National horse). The granite mountains of Britain will soar above the sea, far into the unimaginable future.

DECEMBER

Food in season and local 'sea state' update

Veg
Brussels sprouts, curly kale, garlic, Jerusalem artichokes, chard, spinach

Nuts
Chestnuts

Game
Pheasant, partridge, mallard, grouse, hare, wild rabbit, muntjac, venison

Distance from cliff
19 metres

Change since last month
No change

The House on the Edge

'The house on the edge of the cliff was demolished this week,
which means we are now the house on the edge of the cliff.'

Your News
BBC Radio 4 iPM

TAILPIECE

We live in a windblown house on the edge of an eroding clifftop at the easternmost end of a track which leads only into the sea. The farm track looks as if it wants to continue for a mile or two, but it has been hacked off roughly by the wind and sea and erosion.

Until recently, the presence of the empty house on the edge at the end of our track always acted as a buffer, a bulwark against the inevitability of the encroaching sea. While that house still stood, we felt we had plenty of time. The house on the edge was actually a pair of semis, Weatherly and Four Winds, and its very presence, even with its aura of decrepitude and names hinting at impermanence, was reassuring, much in the way that the presence of older generations of grandparents and parents is reassuring, While they are here, we feel we have plenty of time, but when they go, there is the slight jolt of 'It's us next'.

I nearly bought the house on the edge, for one-tenth of a normal price, with the idea of having nature-loving holidaymakers to stay in one half, thus making my money back in the decade I imagined we might live there, but some reed-cutters appeared out of the mist, like medieval rustic guardian angels and warned me that Covehithe to the north had recently lost sixteen metres in one tide, and I let it go. Some of the lost tourists seem keen to express their opinion that it must be unnerving to live with a short-lease situation, with terms dictated by nature, apparently oblivious that a comparable short lease is literally the only certainty in their own lives, in any of our lives.

One sunny day in June, a cheerful crew of yellow-clad men with yellow machines carefully moved some electricity lines and part of the hedge, and then began to dismantle the house on the edge. The house was probably built in about the 1920s, and was architecturally unremarkable, yet inside it had surprisingly good joinery, doors, fireplaces and staircases etc., and each side had a free-standing claw-footed cast-iron bath. The house was therefore demolished with an eye to selling architectural salvage.

It is a poignant sight to see a house demolished slowly and carefully. Watching the roof tiles being removed was reminiscent of seeing the house during its construction. It was impossible not to imagine the optimism of the fairly recent past, as the house was nearing completion. There is a 1950s photograph of it, spick and span, with car outside, all clearly looked after with pride. Watching the deconstruction of the house, in stop-motion stages punctuated by other normal daily activities, was like watching a film of an unknown people's past memories unravelling, as if a random unlabelled roll of film had been found in some abandoned Museum of Domesticity's attic, its contents alien to one's own family, and outside one's own lifetime, but familiar nevertheless.

As the demolition progressed, the front wall of the house was removed and little rooms appeared like those of a dolls' house. The oppressively domestic scale and nature of the interiors revealed a poignant series of very personal choices, which must once have been made with care and optimism: a cheerful yellow for the bedroom walls, a sky blue here, bright white there ... There was evidence of children having lived in the house and the spirit of the place was one of lightness and happiness and timelessness. Now the yellow digger was bashing straight into that sweet little yellow bedroom, with the indifferent violence of an earthquake in a far-off land, smashing to pieces the foreign country that is the past.

Despite, or perhaps because of, its very ordinariness, I photographed the demolition of the house on the edge for posterity, perhaps for the Southwold Museum archives, perhaps for the local newspaper, perhaps for nobody ever to look at again. I took a series of progress pictures, scientifically arranged from the same spot on the cliff, for several days. Eventually the site was cleared and apart from FOUR WINDS painted in white on a plank nailed to its gatepost, there was no sign of the house on the edge ever having been there at all. No foundations, no pipes, no floors, no bricks, nothing. It was amazing really. The cheerful high-viz men had done a ruthlessly thorough demolition job.

In the process of being recorded for posterity in photographs, the house on the edge of the cliff unwittingly earned a tiny place of permanent posterity in the BBC sound archive, as The House on the Edge of the Cliff. From our few remaining war-generation neighbours up here on our clifftop, we have heard a few verbal recollections of Easton Bavents as it used to be, but rarely is there any visual memory to accompany these stories. The house on the edge of the cliff now has both.

According to local living memory, our track used to continue out to sea up to a rustic T-junction. On the day of the Coronation of the Queen in 1953, people danced in the gardens of cottages which faced the sea, with an east-west front-back arrangement, whereas the remaining cottages face directly south, at right angles to the sea. The lost cottages are clearly marked on our collection of old Ordnance Survey road maps, hoarded not out of any reverence for cartography, but out of our deeply ingrained grandchildren-of-the-war culture of not throwing things away in case they might be useful, which in fact they are. If all that remains of us is what is written down, then the small human story of people dancing in the lost gardens of lost cottages to celebrate the Coronation must be written down, so that the moment remains. The time may have gone and so has the place, but their spirit is here while people still know.

'Send us one sentence of your news this week, and we'll read out a selection on *iPM* to create a little snapshot of Britain,' said Eddie Mair on the kitchen radio as I returned with my photographic bounty. This is a Radio 4 house, and *PM* at 5pm is as familiar a slot as the *Today* programme or the *Shipping Forecast*. So I emailed a sentence and forgot about it:

> 'The house on the edge of the cliff was demolished this week, which means we are now the house on the edge of the cliff.'

A few days later, the telephone rang with a conversation which was noticeably interesting for being neither about PPI insurance nor solar panels:

'Could you collect us from Darsham station, as we'd really like to come and talk about your experience of living with coastal erosion for *iPM* on Radio 4?'

Although we had not heard it, it turned out that the sentence had been read out on Radio 4, along with other little vignettes of people's lives, of dogs, of small plants turning into gigantic trees, and so on, and of such stuff the weekly radio-snapshot of Britain had been made.

On the resulting Radio 4 slot ['Everyone has a cliff edge coming towards them', BBC Radio 4 iPM, 8th August 2015], everything on our cliff seems preserved forever in the immediate moment, in the perpetual-present tense. We walk and talk, and as we walk down the track from our house towards the edge, we count at least fifty paces. We ruminate over the poignancy of the Four Winds sign on the gatepost by a tall hedge. We marvel at the thoroughness of the demolition job, while acknowledging the immediate poignancy of the loss, and we ponder how reassuring it is that we really can leave nothing but footprints, and how this now nice clean cliff will quite soon be in the sea without causing any environmental damage, not quite realising just how soon the whole site could become thin air above the pounding waves.

'Everyone has a cliff coming towards them, in the sense of our time being finite,' I say cheerfully as we tramp about. 'The difference is that we can see ours, pegged out in front of us, so we can say, "When the cliff will be here, we will be about this age."' We walk along the cliff towards the beach, recording live the wild sounds that we still never quite take for granted: the susurration of the sea on the sand; the scrunch of feet on shingle against the screech of a lone gull in the wind; the eerie cries of lapwings and curlews somewhere far away on the crops. The erosion is supposed to average about a metre a year, but of course it goes in fits and starts, and no one can know when it will suddenly be active. That summer, it seemed as if we had plenty of time. Where there were fifty paces, there are now twenty-five.

The thing about it is, though, that when our part of this nature-wrought and romantic place goes, the memory of life here will go with it. Where once Chuffy the Brindle Greyhound bombed about the beach and Cockle the Cockerel gently heralded the dawn with his rural sounds, and our Skyline hens laid beautiful blue eggs, and our vegetable garden thrived, and we loved the place so much, one day, where all that had been, there will be only a particular volume of sky over the sea which will hold all these memories in its air, and the people on the beach below will not know.

www.sandstonepress.com

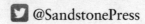 facebook.com/SandstonePress/

@SandstonePress